# What Would Mom Do?

## A Gift from Mom to her
## Adult Child

### By Kathleen Cook

This book is dedicated to my four adult children, who make being a Mom the most precious gift life has ever given me.

# Table of Contents

# Introduction for Moms

## What Will My Kids Do?

I began to think about this book when I was
diagnosed with peripheral artery disease. At the time, two
of my young-adult sons lived with me, both in college.
They focused on work and school while I did all the
"Mom" jobs and operated a home-based business. Neither
of them had any clue as to what my role entailed.

I had failed Parenting 101; I hadn't taught my sons
how to do the laundry, cook, clean or treat minor injuries.
They knew nothing of day-to-day household jobs. Every
week, clean sheets covered their beds as if by magic. When
they sat down to eat, food appeared out of nowhere. I
handled all of the budgeting for the household, so that
appliances miraculously switched on without them having
to think about an electric bill. This was the life that I, as a
woman, had been taught by my mother to live, and I had
passed that notion on to my sons as "normal."

When I received the news of my condition, my first thought was, "How would the boys manage without me?" A few years earlier, relatives would have stepped forward to care for them. Now, my boys would be too proud of their "adult" status to ask for help and everyone would fear interfering, or treating them like children. Yet in some ways, they *were* children.

From that seed sprung this book. I had originally intended to give it to my four grown kids and forget about it, but I thought, "What about other parents like me, who left it too late to teach their kids the life skills they needed to survive without Mom?" This publication is the culmination of that thought. I've added extra blank pages at the end of every section, so that moms across the world can add their own unique instructions for their particular situations. By customizing this book with handwritten notes, you will create your own special version of *What Would Mom Do?* and give your children a treasured and useful memento. If something should happen to you, those handwritten instructions may be the greatest gift you could leave your children.

I suspect that most of us flunk Parenting 101 in one way or another. I read a meme on Facebook the other day that said, "If I managed to keep my kids safe, loved, warm, dry, and well fed until they turned 18, then I consider myself a successful parent." While I had to laugh, I also had to admit that there is so much more to parenting than that. I think I connected most of the dots . . . I did all of the above and tried to provide a good education, talked to them when they needed to talk, and kept a smile on my face even when I was struggling through a gut-wrenching divorce, tending a dying parent and falling apart inside.

Still, I know I skipped over a few of those dots, particularly as a single and overwhelmed mom. This book attempts to retrace my steps and fill in some of those blanks. If you are like me, you may be astonished by the number of things that kids, even adult kids, do not know.

For example, did you ever stop to think that a boy who has never washed a dish will not know to use HOT water? I found that out when I wrote down a list for my son that included, "Fill the sink with water and put the dishes in to soak." He filled it with cold water. No, my son isn't stupid—he was the valedictorian for his high school and went on to obtain an academic college scholarship and graduate with honors. But I had never taught him how to wash dishes.

The things you and I take for granted are the things that our children need to know, especially when they go through something traumatic, whether it is the worst, such as your death, or simply a move across country to obtain a new job or attend college. You may laugh at the cleaning instructions I've included, such as, "After you've swept all the dirt into one small pile on the floor, use the dustpan, which is the plastic tool in the broom closet that looks like a short-handled, wide shovel. Hold it at floor level with one hand and use the broom or brush in the other hand to sweep up all of the dirt. Take the dirt to the trash and then put the dustpan and broom back where they belong."

In this book, I take NOTHING for granted and do not assume that a young adult knows the basics by instinct. I spell them out. The recipes may appear particularly long and complicated, but that is only because each step is painstakingly explained. In reality, they're straightforward and simple. Some instructions will seem like common sense to you, Mom, but if you haven't taught your kids these things, they may not know. If you have, then congratulations. You're a better parent than I and your kids may not need this book.

If you're still reading, then join my club, the "pretty good but not ideal parent" club. No matter how old your adult children are, they can still use this volume to help connect some of those forgotten dots (which is the reason why I chose a cover pic with a somewhat older "young" adult). This book adapts to every adult child's situation, thanks to your supplementation. Long after the printed advice fades into obsolescence, the handwritten instructions will afford both your children and their own offspring a nostalgic legacy.

I hope you live so long that your adult kids never find themselves lost without you, needing your advice and instruction. I hope you enjoy a full life as a carefree senior that they can rely on as their own hair turns gray. But if fate chooses a different path, your kids will thank you for this book.

# Introduction for Adult Children

## What Would Mom Do?

Here you are, launched in life and fully cognizant of your own status as an adult. Wherever you may be, at college, in a new career or simply searching for yourself, there will be times when the "little things" get to you, and you'll wish that Mom were still around to offer a helping hand.

This book attempts to provide that helping hand. It's written in part by YOUR mom, in the handwritten notes that accompany each section. Pay closer attention to those notes than to the printed text, since she knows you better than any anonymous author and can tailor advice specifically to your situation. Understand, also, that she may have better ideas than I do or more expertise on a particular subject. I'm not a master parent; I'm simply a mom with four grown kids who happened to write a book. She could probably write one, too.

Your mom knows that you want to live your life completely on your own, without the nagging and interference that you may have felt during your teen years. She also knows, however, that there will be times when you'll need her guidance, whether you want to acknowledge it or not. This book may save you some embarrassment in having to ask for help.

Some day, Mom won't be around. Try to remember that while she is alive and waiting for a phone call, she'll welcome the opportunity to offer a second opinion in whatever situation you find yourself. Whether she's angry or sad, frightened or annoyed, she is still the very first person who ever loved you, and she always will. Take advantage of that loving concern while she's still around, and make that call.

If your mom is no longer here, treasure the notes that she wrote in this book. Whether they concern a trivial subject, such as where she keeps the pastry brushes, or something serious written in the personal message, remember that she showed her love in every word, every phrase, and every instruction. She wanted you to have a good life; that's why she gave you this book. Now go out and make her proud!

# Chapter One

## Food

### Fast Food and Nutrition

First of all, every adult must learn how to feed themselves. Although you mastered the use of a spoon at only a year old, you may not have thought much about how to put that food on your plate. Now, you must assess your nutritional requirements, food budget, and time constraints.

Many millennials spend too much time in fast food restaurants and not enough time thinking about proper nutrition. While fast food is great when you're pressed for time, you'll eventually have to learn to prepare the bulk of your meals at home. We'll talk about those meals later, but for now, if you really want that fast food, here are the top 10 healthiest fast meals, according to WebMd:

1. Chick-fil-A's Grilled Chicken Sandwich and Fruit Cup
2. Wendy's Baked Potato and Chili Cup

3. KFC's Grilled Chicken Breast, Mashed Potatoes and Corn

4. Chick-fil-A's Chick-n-Minis Breakfast

5. Jack in the Box Chicken Teriyaki Bowl

6. Chick-fil-A's Chargrilled Chicken Cool Wrap

7. McDonald's Southwest Salad and Fruit n Yogurt Parfait

8. Burger King's Veggie Burger and Garden Salad

9. Subway's Veggie Delight Sandwich and Tomato Orzo Soup

10. Taco Bell's Chicken Fresco Burrito Supreme and Pintos 'n' Cheese

Source: http://www.webmd.com/diet/10-best-fast-food-meals?page=1

While I won't tell you that any of these are particularly healthy, since they may still include added salt and unwanted chemicals, they are healthier than what you find in most fast food restaurants.

If you just want to decide what you'll eat once you get to a restaurant, try to frequent fast food places that have generally good food no matter what you order. I like Chipotle because they have eliminated GMOs (genetically modified organisms) from their menu, and in the coming years, that may prove a prophetic decision. Other restaurants include Einstein Bros Bagels, Taco Del Mar, Panera Bread, Noodles and Company, Corner Bakery, and Atlanta Bread. You'll find all of these on Health.com's list of 10 healthiest fast food restaurants. In my humble opinion, these are the cream of the crop, at least of the ones I've visited.

Ultimately, however, nutrition and meals should begin at home. The average person needs about 3.6 grams of carbohydrates and about 1.6 grams of protein per pound of body weight to maintain their condition. Many people nowadays are so worried about fat that they actually consume too little, and wind up gaining more weight than if they had consumed a normal amount. Fat satisfies appetite much more readily than sugars, and will sate your hunger more quickly. Don't be afraid of fat, but don't overdo it, either. Make sure you consume no more than 30 percent of your calories in fat, but not less than 20 percent.

Carbohydrates, too, have gotten a bad rap in recent years. Carbohydrates do not make you fat when consumed responsibly; rather, they are necessary in the healthy maintenance of your body. Be sure to eat a healthy dose of grains, fruits and vegetables daily.

Since this author is an ovo-lacto vegetarian and has acclimated my family to that lifestyle, the printed parts of this book will only contain meatless meals. The handwritten notes that Mom (or Dad) adds, however, may include any type of dish desired.

Still, I urge all people, especially environmentally-conscious young people, to consider the ethics of factory farmed animals, particularly animals whose owners vigorously prosecute anyone who photographs their huge operations. These animals endure horrific conditions before entering the supermarkets of America. While some people still believe that animals feel nothing, most realize that cows and pigs have an awareness equal to that of dogs and cats. If I will not tolerate pet abuse, then I will not "vote with my grocery dollars" for abuse of any other animal. Whatever you decide, however, is up to you, and that is my only word on this subject.

**Basic techniques:**

When I first started making my own meals, breads and jams from scratch, I endured many failures (to which my kids can attest). Nowadays, cooking is routine and I have learned many of the time-tested tips that make things a whole lot easier. As you go through the recipes here, follow the hints and tips and don't be intimidated. After a couple of weeks, you will master skills and have fun in the process.

The recipes I've picked are the things that I know my kids like, and will eat. In the back of each section, your Mom will list her favorite recipes (likely your favorites as well!) Most of my main dishes can be adapted to include meat. Just make certain that it's thoroughly cooked, for safety sake.

Before we start on the recipes, let's review a few tips to make meal preparation easier:

**How to peel vegetables and fruit:**

Use the peeler, a tool found in the kitchen tools drawer that has a slotted single or twin blade and a handle. Hold the vegetable firmly in one hand and the peeler in the other. In peeling a cucumber or a carrot, for example, you would hold the vegetable vertically by the top of the item and place your peeler about half way down. Take your peeler and scrape it firmly against the lower half of the vegetable, in a downward stroke, to peel away a very thin portion of skin. Once you have peeled once, turn the vegetable slightly and then repeat the same motion all the way around the bottom half of the vegetable.

Once you've peeled the entire lower half of the vegetable, turn it around and repeat all the motions with the unpeeled half of the vegetable. By doing it this way, you avoid all chance of the blade scraping your hand. Be careful, because the peeler blade is (or should be) very sharp.

One of the best videos I've seen on the subject is on YouTube by Rebecca Brand, called, "How to Peel and Chop Carrots." You might want to check out her method for peeling:
https://www.youtube.com/watch?v=TPHN52BNCLU

**Peeling tip:** Hold a carrot by the tapered part (nearest the root) and peel the thickest half first. Then turn it around and peel the thick side. If you do it the other way around, you may peel away so much that the thin side will break once you try to hold it to peel the other half.

**Chopping Vegetables:**

When chopping vegetables, remember, SAFETY FIRST. It is not hard to cut yourself if you aren't careful. In fact, it's almost inevitable. Hold your fingers upright and curl them inward, so the blade is pointed away from them. The best video I've seen on this technique is on YouTube by All Recipes called, "Basic Knife Skills." It's about 4 minutes long, and well worth the time spent watching it: https://www.youtube.com/watch?v=Ydc_SaQ_eRQ

**Veggie tip:** Check the bar code sticker on your fruits and veggies. If the bar code number starts with a "9," the produce is organic.

## Storage times for various items:

**Bread:** On the counter, home-baked bread will last 3 days. Store bought loaves may stay fresh longer, since they contain preservatives not found in your own bread. In the fridge, you can keep bread 5 days, but the taste is better if you don't refrigerate. You can freeze extra bread for up to 3 months, as long as you wrap it well. Check my bread recipe in the grains section for instructions on wrapping.

**Oil:** Oil in the pantry will last about 3 months after it's opened. You can put oil in the fridge to lengthen that time, but it may turn cloudy. That will not affect the taste or appearance once your food is cooked.

**Butter:** This will last about 2 weeks in the fridge, but you can easily freeze extra butter, wrapped well, for up to a year.

**Cheese** will last anywhere from 2 weeks to 3 months in the fridge, depending upon the brand. Hard cheeses, like cheddar, last much longer than soft ones, such as mozzarella. You can freeze almost any cheese, but remember, freezing will affect texture and possibly taste. I find that gouda lasts a long time in the freezer and the texture is not much different than fresh.

**Meals:** Home made or purchased frozen meals will last about 3 months in the freezer, if wrapped.

### Storing Eggs:

How do you tell if eggs are good? Submerge an egg into water . If it jumps up and floats, it must be thrown away. If it stands up but doesn't rise, it is good enough for cooking, but don't use it fresh for anything, such as egg nog. If it lays flat under the water and doesn't stand up, it's perfect.

How do you tell if an egg is fresh or hard boiled? I've experienced that problem before; I've hard boiled eggs and then accidentally mixed them in with my fresh eggs.

To tell the difference without cracking it open, just spin it. If it spins easily with no wobble, it's cooked. If it wobbles as it spins, it's raw.

Eggs can keep 4-5 weeks in the fridge. You'll probably hear that Europeans don't refrigerate their eggs, but that's only because commercial egg breeders there don't wash off the egg's natural barrier. American eggs must be washed before selling, and that destroys the protective coating. Therefore, American eggs must be refrigerated.

For all other items, check the expiration date, but don't be intimidated by it. For some goods, the expiration dates are a guideline and quite often, food is still  good after that date. This holds true for both dry foods and unopened canned and bottled goods. However, don't bother with anything that's long past its expiration date. Better safe than sorry.

**Measurements and Terms:**

Use measuring spoons and cups when measuring out portions in recipes. These are different from the tablespoons and teaspoons that we use to eat our food, or the coffee cups we grab in the morning. Whenever a "teaspoon" (tsp) or "tablespoon" (tbsp) is mentioned in the cooking section, it means a measuring spoon.

A "heaping" spoonful is a measuring spoon that is filled as much as possible. In other words, stick the spoon into the substance, such as sugar, and then scoop up as much as the spoon will hold. That's a heaping spoonful, whether it is a heaping tablespoon, heaping teaspoon, etc.

A "rounded" spoonful is a little less than a heaping spoonful. You dip it into the substance and then shake it a little bit so that it's not piled quite as high as a heaping teaspoon, but still a generous spoonful.

A "level" spoonful is completely level with the spoon. You achieve this by dipping the spoon into the substance and then taking a knife or other edge and sliding it across the spoon, so that the substance you are measuring sits only in the oval well of the spoon, not above it. When you are sliding the knife across the spoon, make sure you are holding it above the box or bag of substance you are measuring, so that you don't waste that extra bit, which can be used next time.

"Mince" means to chop so finely that it is difficult if not impossible to pick up an individual piece of food. "Dice" means to chop in very small pieces but not quite as small as mincing. You can easily pick up an individual piece. When a "pinch" of something is called for, this is a very small amount, such as the amount you can get between your thumb and forefinger easily. Likewise, a dash is a similar amount, but just a tiny bit more than a pinch, perhaps an 1/8th of a level teaspoon.

**Note:** The term "oven" in this book means a regular bake oven. "Toaster oven" is the appliance that works like a bake oven, but is smaller. "Microwave" is used when talking about a microwave oven. The latter can be used to heat food quickly.

**CAUTION:** Never, ever put anything plastic into a regular oven OR a toaster oven. While you may place plastic in microwaves, you CANNOT do that with regular or toaster ovens! Use only metal utensils or other items designed for baking, such as baking stones, glass, parchment paper, etc.

**One more tip:** Do not use metal utensils on a non-stick pan or griddle. Use only plastic pancake turners or spoons, etc. Metal utensils will scratch the non-stick coating off of the pan, leaving it much more difficult to clean.

**More Kitchen Tips from Mom:**

# Main Dishes

While it's better and healthier to make main dishes from scratch, there are times when you will want to simply pop a store-bought frozen meal into the oven. For those times, please choose wisely. Here are some of the healthiest brands of frozen meals, according to Health.com:

Evol Fire-Grilled Steak

Luvo Chicken Chile Verde

Kashi Mayan Harvest Bake

Saffron Road Chicken Biryani

Saffron Road Chana Saag

Lean Cuisine Spa Collection Sesame Stir Fry

Cedar Lane Eggplant Parmesan

Luvo Spinach Ricotta Ravioli

Blake's Meatloaf Dinner Casserole

Artisan Bistro Grass-Fed Beef in Mushroom Sauce

Luvo Orange Mango Chicken

Artisan Bistro Wild Salmon with Pesto

Kashi Steam Meal Chicken Chipotle BBQ

Note that in the above list, most contain meat. For ovo-lacto vegetarians like me, I can attest to the fact that the Mayan Harvest Bake, the Chana Saag and the Eggplant Parmesan are wonderful.

When you have time to cook, however, making your own meals can be healthier and more satisfying. If you find yourself with a free afternoon, cook in bulk and then freeze the leftovers for another day, thus avoiding the expense of frozen packaged meals.

Let's start with an easy "50/50" soup, which means that 50 percent of it is made up of a commercial soup base and 50 percent is made up of added "scratch" ingredients. When you're in a hurry and don't want to make a full blown meal, a 50/50 compromise may be the best thing.

### 50/50 Hearty Soup

Yield: about 2 quarts

Ingredients:
1 box Pacific Organic Roasted Red Pepper Tomato Soup
(or any canned or boxed tomato soup)
1 potato or small zucchini, diced

1 carrot, diced

1 stalk of celery, sliced thinly

½ onion, sliced thinly

1 tbsp olive or coconut oil

2 tbsp chopped basil leaves

1 tbsp grated cheese


Utensils Needed:

Pot

Frying pan

Spatula

Grater

Large Spoon

Chopping knife


Wash your veggies and then slice or dice them into small pieces (approximately ½" cubes or slices). Heat 1 tbsp of oil in a skillet on medium high heat, and then add your diced carrots. Cook them for about 2 minutes, then add your potato (or zucchini), celery and onion and cook until soft and slightly browned, which may take anywhere from 2 to 4 additional minutes, depending upon the size of the pieces.

Open your box of tomato soup and pour into a pot. Add your cooked veggies and chopped basil, and simmer for a few minutes until hot and starting to bubble, but not burned. Sprinkle the grated cheese on top and serve with biscuits. (You'll find an easy biscuit recipe in the Grains section of this book.)

If you have more time, here are a few main dishes that are healthy and hearty:

**Veggie Burritos**

Yield: 3-4 burritos

Ingredients:
Tortillas (see recipe in the Grains section, or buy them)
1 Bell Peppers (red, green, yellow or orange)
1/2 medium onion or a few green onions
1 stalk of celery
Salsa (See recipe below)
Any non-GMO cooking oil
4 ounces of cheese, pre-shredded
fresh or dried rosemary or basil, if desired

Utensils needed:

1 large skillet

1 spatula or large spoon

Knife for chopping veggies

Cutting Board

**1.** Wash the veggies. Chop the onion, celery and bell pepper into bite-sized pieces.

**2.** Chop a couple of sprigs of rosemary (about 10 individual needles) or a few basil leaves finely, or use half a teaspoon of dried rosemary or basil, if desired.

**3.** Heat 2 tablespoons of oil in a skillet on medium-high. Drop all of the veggies into the hot oil and stir them with a spatula. Add the herbs or, if you choose, add meat or fish if desired. Cook for approximately 3 minutes or until glistening but still a bit firm. (Taste them and see if they taste "done" to you.)

**4.** Turn off the heat and place a couple of spoonfuls of veggies on the center of a tortilla. Add a spoonful of grated cheese. Pour about 1 tablespoon (or more if you prefer) salsa over the filling.

**6.** Fold over the sides of the tortilla, then roll it up to form a burrito. Place two burritos per plate. Place the burritos in a microwave for 30-45 seconds to melt the cheese and serve.

## Fresh Salsa for the Burritos

This recipe can be used for any foods requiring a spicy salsa, such as Taco Salad (see recipe later in this section).

Ingredients:

1 teaspoon lemon juice

1 teaspoon sugar or agave syrup

⅛ tsp salt

½ tsp Italian seasoning OR 2 teaspoons fresh basil, if desired

1 Jalapeno pepper, chopped

2 slices of cucumber, chopped

1 small tomato, chopped

½ bell pepper, chopped

1 stalk of green onion or ⅛ cup of regular onion, chopped

Utensils:

Measuring cup, ⅛

Measuring spoons, ⅛, ½, and 1 teaspoon

Blender

Add all ingredients to the blender and blend until it is the consistency you want in salsa. Chunky salsa will require only about 20 seconds of blending; a thinner salsa may require a minute. You can make it either spicier or less spicy by adding or reducing the jalapeno.

## Quesadillas

(This is a great way to use leftover tortillas that have gotten a bit dried out and crack too easily for burritos.)

Yield: 8 quarter pieces

Ingredients:
2 large Tortillas (see recipe)
4 ounces cheese, previously shredded
Grape seed, coconut or olive oil

Optional Ingredients:
Fresh or dried herbs, such as basil or rosemary
Salsa, if desired (see recipe, above)

Utensils needed:
cookie sheet

pizza cutter

pastry brush

chopping knife

**1.** Set oven for 400 degrees

**2.** Cut tortillas into quarters to make 8 pieces.

**3.** Brush a small amount of oil (1 teaspoon) on the cookie sheet with a pastry brush; make sure the oil is evenly coated. Or as an alternative, use parchment paper to line the cookie sheet.

**4.** Place the tortilla pieces on the cookie sheets and arrange them in any configuration that will fit. Sprinkle shredded cheese generously on the tortillas. Sprinkle a small amount of herbs, if desired. (About a rounded teaspoon of total herbs distributed between all pieces.)

**5.** Put the trays in the oven and bake for between 4-6 minutes. After four minutes, watch the tortillas carefully to make certain that they do not burn. Once the cheese is bubbling and starting to turn very light brown (not dark), they are done. They will be soft when first taken out of the oven but will firm up as they cool.

**6.** Eat them plain or add salsa to them. Store any leftovers very tightly wrapped.

# Pizza

Yield: Makes 1 large pizza or 2 medium pizzas

Ingredients for Dough

2 cups of All Purpose Flour (plus extra for dusting the pizza dough)

1 level tablespoon of sugar

1 level teaspoon salt

Approximately 1 cup of water

1 rounded tablespoon of instant dry yeast (see tips on yeast)

Optional:

1 tablespoon of finely chopped basil, rosemary or other herbs

Pizza Toppings:

⅓ jar of any spaghetti sauce

6-12 ounces of shredded cheese

Chopped green peppers, onions, green onions, celery, mushrooms, olives, tomatoes, or any other pizza toppings of your choice.

Utensils needed:

Large Bowl

Large wooden cutting board

Wire cooling rack

Large Cookie Sheet

Mixing Spoon

Measuring cup

Rolling Pin

Measuring spoons: tablespoon and teaspoon

Pizza Cutter

Pastry brush

Parchment Paper (the kind that comes in rolls, not sheets, unless you like that particular size for pizza)

Oven Mitt

**1.** Put a cup of water into the microwave for 25-30 seconds. It should be warm but not hot, or it will kill the yeast.

**2.** In a large bowl, mix the yeast, flour, sugar, and salt, making sure to stir after each ingredient Add the water, up to a cup as needed. Mix to make a very soft dough. If the dough is stiff, add more water. If too watery, add more flour sparingly. Better for the dough to be too soft than not soft enough.

**3.** Pick up the dough and knead it lightly for about 2 minutes, to distribute the gluten. Put it back in the bowl and cover the bowl with plastic wrap. You can put it in a cold oven, to avoid drafts, and turn on the light, but NOT the oven itself. Set timer for 30 minutes.

**4.** When the dough is ready to work, take it out and then set the oven to 450 (very hot) degrees.

**5.** While the oven is preheating, cut off a piece of parchment paper that is about the size of your wire cooling rack, the one that you'll place your pizza shell on. Do not confuse this wire cooling rack with the wire oven rack, which is one of two big ones that stay in the oven at all times. The cooling rack is smaller, but of similar design.

NOTE: I realize this is confusing, but you will actually bake your pizza on the cooling rack that will sit directly on top of the oven rack. Even though it's called a "cooling" or "cake" rack, you can bake a pizza on it. The reason you use this "double rack" method is so you can easily place your pizza in the oven while the dough is soft and raw, but still allow air to circulate under the pizza during baking. (The parchment paper will not prohibit air flow as a cookie sheet would.) Using this method, the crust is firm and crusty, as good pizza should be.

If you have a large cooling rack, you can make one large pizza. If you only have smaller racks, you can make two medium pizzas (on two pieces of parchment paper.)

**6.** Sprinkle flour all over the parchment paper. (Yes, I know that parchment paper is not supposed to need it, but trust me on this.) Place your dough ball (or half of the dough, if you are making two pizzas) onto the parchment paper and press it down to flatten the dough. Sprinkle flour on top of the dough and then roll it with a rolling pin to almost fit the size of the paper. If the dough sticks to the rolling pin, sprinkle flour on it.

**7.** Once your pizza shell is spread out to the desired size on the parchment paper, slide the dough (with the parchment paper still under it) onto the cooling rack. Open the oven door and place the cooling rack holding your pizza shell on the oven rack. Position it on the lower oven rack and close the door. Set the timer for about 8 minutes, depending upon your oven.

**8.** While the pizza shell is cooking, you can chop any toppings that you like. Wash fresh vegetables, if you are using them. You may slice mushrooms, olives, green peppers, hot peppers, celery, onions, tomatoes, etc. Also, grate enough cheese to cover the pizza, about 8-10 ounces of cheese. Use your own judgment.

**9.** When the pizza shell is done, pull out the wire cooling rack on which your pizza shell sits (use oven mitts!) Place it on the top of the stove or on a protected mat on the counter (don't place a hot rack directly on a counter.) Keep the oven on but close the door. (If the timer automatically shuts off the oven, as in my old stove, you'll have to immediately turn the oven back up to 450 degrees.) Pull the parchment paper out from under the pizza shell and discard it, but leave the pizza on the rack.

**10.** Create your pizza by first spreading spaghetti sauce, then grated cheese, then any toppings that you've chosen, and then more grated cheese at the end, to hold all the toppings onto the pizza. Add your herbs/spices, if you wish. (Basil, oregano, etc.)

**11.** Once your pizza is topped, place it (still on the wire rack) into the oven and bake for 8-10 minutes. Remember to place the pizza on the lower oven rack, so that it will cook well on the bottom.

**12.** When the bottom is cooked and the pizza cheese is nice and bubbly, take the rack out of the oven (using mitts) and slide the pizza onto a large wooden cutting board. Cut into pieces with a pizza cutter.

# Taco Salad

Yield: As much as or little as you like

Ingredients: (in whatever quantities you like I usually use about ¼ cup of each ingredient per person.)

Tortilla Chips

Lettuce, shredded

Tomatoes, chopped

Bell Peppers, chopped

Carrots, sliced

Onions, chopped

Cucumbers, sliced

Mushrooms, sliced

Salsa (see recipe above)

Ranch Dressing

One can of chili, your favorite

Grated cheese

Utensils needed:

Knife for dicing and slicing

Peeler for peeling carrots and cucumbers

**1.** Wash all vegetables under running water thoroughly.

**2.** Chop, slice or dice all veggies. (Make sure you peel the cucumbers before slicing them.)

**3.** Open the can of chili, pour into a bowl and heat in the microwave for 60 seconds.

**4.** To make a salad on each individual plate, first place tortilla chips as the bed for the salad. Use anywhere from 12-20 chips, depending on personal preference. Then pour chili over the chips, and afterwards, add any desired veggies. Top with cheese, salsa and ranch dressing, as desired.

### Spaghetti

Yield: Enough for 3 or 4 people

Ingredients:

1 package (16 ounces) spaghetti (If there are only two people, use a 12 ounce package, or a partial package for 1 person, and halve the amount of veggies.)

1 jar (26 ounces) spaghetti sauce

2 stalks celery, chopped

½ onion, chopped

1 bell pepper, chopped

1 sprig of rosemary, a few basil leaves, or any other herbs
that you like, such as a half teaspoon of oregano.

2 tablespoons oil for fry pan

1 teaspoon of oil for the large pot

½ teaspoon of salt (optional)

Small amount of shredded cheese


Utensils needed:

Large pot for boiling the spaghetti

Skillet for frying

Spatula

Knife for chopping

Extra long Spoon for stirring spaghetti

Colander

Tongs

measuring spoons


**1.** Fill a large pot ¾ full with water and place on stove.
Turn up the heat to "high" to boil the water. This will take
10-20 minutes depending upon the size of the pot.

**2.** While you are waiting for the water to boil, chop the
celery, onion and bell pepper. Put the oil in a fry pan and
coat the pan evenly by tilting it back and forth until the oil

covers the bottom of the pan. Place it on a burner and turn the heat to medium high. Once the oil is hot, add the chopped vegetables to the skillet. Chop the herbs and add them in, or use a half teaspoon of dried herbs.

**3.** As soon as the veggies are cooked but still crunchy (about3 minutes), add the jar of spaghetti sauce and a bit of shredded cheese and stir everything together. Turn down the heat to "simmer" or "low," and let it gently cook, stirring occasionally.

**4.** When the water in the large pot is boiling (rapidly bubbling), add a teaspoon of oil to the water and a ½ teaspoon of salt, if desired. This will help to prevent the water from boiling over, and will also season the pasta. Open the package of spaghetti and pour it into the pot. Stir the pieces so that they all wind up under the water; don't leave any pieces sticking up out of the water. That way, they can boil evenly.

**5.** Cook the spaghetti for about 7 to 8 minutes. Stir every couple of minutes to make certain that the spaghetti does not burn on the bottom of the pot.

**6.** Once the spaghetti is done (taste a small strand to make sure) then place the colander in an empty, clean sink. CAREFULLY take the pot of water to the sink and pour it SLOWLY into the colander. Boiling water is dangerous, so take your time to pour slowly so the water does not splash on you and so that it does not back up through the drain of the sink and contaminate the food.

Once most of the water is drained, let the spaghetti fall directly into the colander. Shake the colander gently to remove any excess water. Then pour the spaghetti into a serving dish.

**7.** To eat your spaghetti, take the spaghetti noodles out with tongs and place on plate, then top with the spaghetti sauce/veggie mixture from the skillet.

## Veggie Casserole

Yield: Enough for 3-4 people for a main course

Ingredients:

1 bell pepper

1 onion

2 stalks of celery

1 or 2 tomatoes

Other veggies, as desired (sliced thin carrots, corn, etc.)

Fresh herbs, if desired

4 to 6 ounces of cheese

1 package (12 or 16 ounces) pasta (Fuseli, Rotini, Macaroni or other short pieces of pasta.)
1 to 2 tablespoons of non-GMO oil, plus a dash of oil for the boiling pot.
Salt for the boiling pot

Utensils needed:
Large Pot
Colander
Large spoon
Frying pan
Chopping knife

**1.** Fill a large pot half-way full with water and heat on high heat. Let the water boil, then add a dash of oil and salt to the water before adding the package of pasta. Boil for about 6-10 minutes depending upon the kind of pasta it is. Macaroni takes the shortest; the squiggly varieties like Fuseli take the longest. Taste to see if it is soft enough for you, and if it is, take it immediately off the heat and drain in a colander. Don't leave it in the water, or it will get mushy.

**2.** Chop and dice the onion, pepper, tomatoes, celery and any other veggies you might want in this. If you use carrots, make sure they are sliced very thinly or they won't cook thoroughly. Heat the oil in a skillet on medium high. Once it is hot, add your veggies and cook for about 3-4 minutes. Add fresh herbs, one or two teaspoons chopped, if you wish. (If you use dried herbs from the bottles, use only half that amount.)

**3.** When the veggies are done, add the drained pasta to the skillet and then top with the cheese. Mix thoroughly. If you wish, you may add spaghetti sauce to the mixture to make it more saucy.

**Variation:** If you want to have an Oriental-style meal, then leave out the tomatoes and the pasta as well as the cheese. Instead of the pasta, cook white rice (see recipe). To the veggie mixture, add bamboo shoots or water chestnuts (found in the Oriental food section of the store, in small cans). You may even add pineapple, if you wish. When you have your veggie mixture and your rice both done, then place the rice on your plate and spoon the veggie mixture over it. You may top it with chow mein noodles, also found in the Oriental food section. Add soy sauce, if desired.

# Gloomkies Casserole

Gloomkies is a funny word that my Lithuanian mother used for cabbage rolls. It's a traditional nickname in both Ukranian and Lithuanian cultures and it's a good way to get your veggies, especially veggies you may not like, such as cabbage. You may add half a pound of THOROUGLY cooked hamburger meat, if you are not vegetarian. This recipe will be enough for several people, so freeze the excess if you're alone.

This recipe changes traditional gloomkies into a casserole, and is much easier to prepare since you don't have to "roll" anything. You just stir all the ingredients together, and it comes out tasting pretty much the same.

Ingredients:
1/2  head cabbage
2 cups cooked white rice (see recipe)
1 jar of spaghetti sauce
One half of an onion, chopped (or 3 stalks of green onion)
2 stalks of celery, sliced
1 large bell pepper, chopped
6 ounces of cheese

Herbs from the garden (3 or four basil leaves, chopped, and one spring of rosemary, chopped, or any dried versions.)
Non-GMO Oil, 1 or 2 tablespoons


Utensils needed:

Saucepan large enough to hold a head of cabbage, shredded

Large pot

Large bowl

Frying pan

Large spoon

Measuring cup

Colander


**1.** Cook the rice per the instructions in the recipe (included later in this book) and set aside.

**2.** Bring a saucepan half filled with water to a boil. Chop the cabbage into small pieces and submerge in the hot water. Boil it for five minutes.

**3.** While you are waiting for the cabbage to cook, chop all your veggies and herbs into small, bite-sized pieces.

**4.** Heat a fry pan on medium high heat and add 1 or 2 tablespoons of oil. Add all the veggies and herbs (except for the cabbage) to the frying pan and fry for about 3 minutes, or until the veggies are glistening. Turn off the heat.

**5.** Add the rice to the veggie mixture. Stir in one-half of the spaghetti sauce and all of the cheese. Mix thoroughly.

**6.** Drain the cabbage from the boiling water and add it to the rice and veggies and stir well.

**8.** Pour the last half of the spaghetti sauce over the top of the cabbage casserole. Sprinkle more cheese on the top.

**9.** Cover the fry pan with a lid and put it in a 350 degree oven. Bake for about 45 minutes.

**TIP:** Make sure your frying pan is the kind that can do "double duty" and go into the oven. If it can't, then bake your casserole in a separate oven-safe dish.

### Mom's Best Zucchini Casserole

(Makes enough for 4 people, or you can freeze leftovers for anytime. This is easier than it looks. The reason for so many steps is simply the layering process.)

Ingredients
2 zucchinis, fresh
1- 12 ounce package of Rotini or Macaroni (or other pasta)

1 package of Red Hot Blues tortilla chips (organic), or any tortilla chips of your choice

½ lb of cheese, shredded or grated

10 fresh basil leaves

1 bunch of green onions

1 jar of Spaghetti sauce

Dash of oil and salt for the boiling pot

Utensils:

Baking pan (or "bake-able" frying pan) with lid

Large pot for boiling pasta.

Chopping knife

**1.** Fill a large pot half-way full with water and heat on high. Let the water boil, then add a dash of oil and salt before adding the package of pasta. Boil for about 6-10 minutes depending upon the type of pasta. Macaroni takes the shortest; the squiggly varieties like Fuseli take the longest. Taste to see if it is soft enough for you, and if it is, take it immediately off the heat and drain in a colander. Don't leave it in the water or it will get mushy.

**2.** Wash and peel the zucchinis. Slice the zucchinis thinly (about ¼" to ⅓" thick pieces) and then set aside. Wash the green onions and then chop only the green parts very thinly. Save the white parts for any other recipe that requires onions. Wash and chop the basil leaves and mix them together with the green onion in a bowl.

**3.** After the pasta is cool, prepare your assembly line of ingredients in this order: Jar of pasta sauce, bowl of zucchini, Red Hot Blues chips, bowl of green onions/basil, bowl of pasta, bowl of shredded cheese.

**4.** Pour about ⅓ of the spaghetti sauce into the bottom of the baking pan and layer about ½ of the zucchini slices over the top of the sauce.

**5.** Crush two or three handfuls of tortilla chips over the zucchini slices. Use more or less as desired.

**6.** Sprinkle about half of the basil leaves/green onion mixture over the top of the tortilla chips, and then add half of the cooked pasta.

**7.** Top the whole mixture with about half of the cheese.

**10.** Repeat all layers one time, in the same order, using ⅓ of the pasta sauce, the last half of zucchini, three more handfuls of chips, the rest of the green onions/basil, the rest of the pasta, and the rest of the cheese.

**11.** Finish with the last ⅓ of spaghetti sauce. Cover and bake at 350 degrees for 50 minutes to 1 hour.

# Vegetarian Bean Burgers

Yield: Makes 4 burgers

Ingredients:

¾ cup of rolled oats (old fashioned kind)

1 can of kidney, black or pinto beans

2 tablespoons chopped basil leaves

½ teaspoon of salt

2 tablespoons homemade salsa (see recipe earlier in this section)

1 egg, beaten

⅓ cup chopped green onions

1 clove of garlic, minced very fine (Note, a "clove" is only one tiny section of a bulb of garlic. If you pull apart a garlic bulb, you will find, normally, 8-10 cloves within it.)

1 teaspoon lemon or lime juice

Utensils needed:

Griddle

Food Processor or Blender

Spatula

Mixing Bowl and spoon

Waxed Paper

Cookie Sheet


Grind oats in a food processor or blender for about
30 seconds and then put in a mixing bowl. Add all the
liquid ingredients together (egg, salsa and juice) and pour
over the oats, then throw in the garlic, salt, basil and beans.
Mix everything thoroughly and then form into 3 or 4
patties.

Line a cookie sheet with waxed paper and place
your patties on the paper and slide them into EITHER the
freezer for about 5 minutes, or the refrigerator for about 15,
wherever you have the room. While the patties are cooling,
heat up your griddle.

Add about 1 tablespoon of olive oil to your griddle
and then place each pattie with a spatula carefully on the
griddle, so that it doesn't fall apart. Cook on one side for
about 6-8 minutes, then turn them with the spatula to the
other side for an additional 6 or 7 minutes. Serve just like
you would a hamburger pattie, with a bun or crumble in a
salad to substitute for meat.

# Your Mom's Main Dishes

_____

_____

_____

_____

_____

_____

_____

_____

# Sides, Sandwiches and Snacks

## Easy Baked French Fries

Baking French fries is a lot healthier than frying them, and a lot easier than dealing with the oil mess.

Yield: 2 servings

Ingredients:
2 large potatoes
2 tablespoons oil
seasonings to taste (dash of salt, pepper, herbs, etc.)

Utensils needed:
cookie sheet
Parchment Paper
Knife for slicing
Potato Peeler
Oven Mitt

**1.** Preheat oven to 400 degrees

**2.** Peel potatoes and then cut into slices about ⅓" thick. Take each slice and cut lengthwise into French fry-sized pieces, if desired. Put all pieces into a bowl.

**3.** Pour 2 tablespoons of oil over the potatoes and mix well so that all potato pieces are coated with oil.

**4.** Roll out parchment paper large enough to cover the cookie sheet. Spread the paper over the cookie sheet with the curved side down, to keep it in place.

**5.** Spread potatoes evenly over the parchment paper-lined cookie sheets. Sprinkle salt and other seasonings over the potatoes as desired.

**6.** Bake at 400 for about 20 minutes until lightly browned. Check often to avoid burning. When they are lightly browned, take the cookie sheet out of the oven with an oven mitt and place on the top of the stove. Carefully pick up the parchment paper piece on both sides, slide the French fries into a bowl or onto a plate and eat while hot.

## Basic White Cooked Rice

(Makes about 2 cups of cooked rice)

Ingredients

1 cup of rice

2 cups of water

1 tsp lemon juice

¼ tsp salt

Utensils:

Measuring spoon

Measuring cup

heavy saucepan with lid (such as a cast iron saucepan)

long spoon (such as a wooden stirring spoon)

**1.** Place 2 cups of water, 1 teaspoon of lemon juice and a quarter teaspoon of salt in a medium saucepan and heat on "high" heat. At the same time as you do this, turn another burner on to the "low" setting, so that it will be warming while your water is heating on the "high" burner.

**2.** Once the water boils very vigorously (with steam rising and rapidly bubbling water, about 3-5 minutes), add one cup of dry rice to the water. After you add the rice, stir it to distribute the rice evenly throughout the water and then put the lid on the pan. Transfer the pan to the new burner on the "low" setting and then cook at "low" for about 15-18 minutes.

**Rice Trick:** If you have a very heavy cast iron saucepan with a tight fitting lid, you can omit the second burner in the recipe above. Once you add the rice to the pan, stir it and then put on the lid, you may simply turn the heat down to "low" and cook for an additional 15 minutes. That only works with thick, cast iron pans. Thin pans will cause the rice to boil over if you leave it on the same burner.

**TIPS ON RICE:** Short grain rice is starchier. I find it cooks faster but also sticks together more. Long grain rice doesn't stick as much but takes a bit longer to cook (and it's usually more expensive.) Note that brown rice will take **three times as long** to cook as white, and you will have to vary the amounts of water/rice to achieve a good result. You may add herbs, sugar, or anything else to rice.

### Grilled Sandwiches

Yield: Makes two sandwiches

Ingredients:
4 slices of bread
4 ounces of cheese
2 tablespoons of coconut or any other oil

Any of the following: tomato slices, cucumber slices, chopped fresh herbs, sliced onions, hot peppers
Salt (optional)

Utensils:
Griddle
Spatula
Knife
Pastry brush

**1.** Heat the griddle to the highest setting.

**2.** Brush one side of each slice of bread with coconut oil. You may also use coconut butter, if you prefer, and spread it with a knife, or even margarine.

**3.** Slice the cheese into thin slices and slice any vegetables thinly.

**4.** Once the griddle is hot, place two slices of bread on the griddle, oiled side down. Add the slices of cheese and any veggies or herbs that you have chosen, layered on top of the bread. Add a light sprinkle of salt, if desired. Place the remaining slice of bread on top of each sandwich with the oiled side up.

**5.** Let cook for 2-3 minutes, then turn each sandwich with the spatula to cook the other side. This takes some practice.

Hold the top of the sandwich with your hand as you flip, in order to keep it from falling apart. If you can't manage it, you can take a large pair of tongs and hold the sandwich together with the tongs while you are flipping it. In time, this will get easy.

**6.** Cook on the flipped side for another 2 minutes or until browned as desired.

## Eggs

FRIED EGGS: Brush a tablespoon of oil onto a griddle and heat it on high. Once it's hot, crack the egg onto the hot griddle, cook for one minute, then flip it over and cook for another minute on the other side.

BOILED EGGS: Fill a medium saucepan with cold water about ¾ full. Place the eggs into the cold water and then put the saucepan on the stove and heat on high. (Make sure you don't drop fresh eggs into hot water; they might crack from the heat. Both water and eggs must heat together.) Once the water starts boiling (bubbling rapidly) set the timer for 4-5 minutes. Once the timer goes off, take the eggs off the heat and let them cool off gently. If you are in a hurry, you can pull the eggs out of the water with tongs and place them in a bowl of ice water. They will cool down faster that way.

SCRAMBLED EGGS: Crack open two or more eggs into a bowl. Add a tablespoon of milk and a pinch of salt for every two eggs. If you wish, you may add herbs or finely chopped veggies. Stir mixture vigorously. Take out a skillet and oil it with a small amount of oil. Heat the pan on medium high, and once it's hot, pour your egg mixture into the pan. Keep stirring until it congeals, which will take a couple minutes. Once the eggs are thick and congeal into small clumps, turn off the heat and pour your eggs onto a plate.

### Fresh Fruit Jam

Yield: 1 large jar of "refrigerator" jam, to be used within 3 weeks. Do not store this jam on a pantry shelf.

Ingredients:
2 lbs of fresh fruit, peeled and shredded (or 2 packages frozen fruit, chopped into bite-sized pieces (berries, apples, stone fruits and oranges all work great, but avoid pineapple and kiwi if you are a novice)

Pomona's Universal Pectin (or any low-sugar or no-sugar pectin)

1/3 cup lime juice (or lemon)

Any amount of sugar you wish, from none to 4 tablespoons.

Utensils needed:

2 quart saucepan with lid

Wooden spoon for stirring

Small container (any small, clean bottle with a cap will do. It must hold one cup.)

Clean jar, such as a peanut butter jar with metal lid

Small bowl

fork (any)

**1.** Open the universal pectin box. You'll see a small packet and a larger packet. Take the small packet (the calcium packet) and pour it into a small container with a tight-fitting cap. Add one cup of water, close the cap and shake. You'll need only a small amount of this mixture, so store the rest in the fridge for later jam batches. It will last for at least six months. (I like to use empty plastic water bottles to store my calcium water, but just make sure you label it carefully so no one accidentally drinks it.)

**2.** Peel your fruit and then shred it with a grater (use the side of the grater that has the largest holes). Place the shredded fruit in the saucepan and add as much or as little sugar as you wish, if any. Stir until the sugar is distributed and then heat the fruit on medium high heat and cook until the fruit is very soft and is bubbling. Be careful not to scorch the fruit.

**3.** While the fruit cooks, microwave ⅓ cup of lime or lemon juice in the small bowl for about 30 seconds.

**4.** Open the larger packet in the pectin box and spoon out about one teaspoon of the powder. (Save the rest of the packet for another time.) Add it to the warm lime or lemon juice and stir quickly with a fork, to avoid lumps. Add one teaspoon of the calcium water that you made in step one. Once the mixture is stirred and fairly smooth, add it to the hot fruit in the saucepan and stir vigorously.

**5.** Let the fruit mixture continue to cook and bubble, stirring it to avoid burning and to incorporate the pectin, for at least two more minutes, then turn off the stove and remove the pan from the heat. Cover with a lid and leave it alone for 30 minutes, to finish cooking without added heat.

**6.** When the jam is cool enough to handle, stir it well and pour into any clean jar (I like to use my old peanut butter jars with metal lids). Store the jam in the refrigerator; it will last approximately three weeks.

**Tip:** You must use pectin **specifically** made for low-sugar recipes. If you try to use the regular, high-sugar pectin, this recipe will not work. You can double the recipe without doubling the pectin. Use 50 percent more pectin (and calcium water) with twice the amount of fruit, to save money. However, remember that this is not canned jam, and will not keep on a shelf. You must use it within three weeks and keep it in your fridge, so make only the amount you can use or give away.

## Your Mom's Side Dishes

_____

_____

_____

_____

_____

# Grains

Grains and other carbohydrates are important for maintaining healthy bodies. They are low in calorie density, provide key nutrients, and most importantly, reduce our chances of heart attack and stroke. As a bonus, they are good for the planet. To produce the same amount of protein value in our diet, beef requires twenty times as much fossil fuel. In this era of climate change awareness, that simply isn't sustainable.

If you have a wheat or gluten allergy, I suggest you try either Einkorn or Emmer Wheat Flour. These are ancient forms of wheat that cause far fewer allergic reactions than our modern wheat. They still contain gluten, but the gluten is different and may be tolerated by those who react negatively to modern flours (as I do.) My favorite place to buy Einkorn flour is through Vitacost, but you may also find it on Amazon or in a specialty grocer. While it does cost more than mass-produced, modern wheat, for those with gluten intolerance it can be a lifesaver, since it rises nearly as well as modern wheat and allows many gluten sufferers to enjoy pizza, tortillas, and bread.

Since I live in the desert, my recipes are adapted to the desert. Here in Phoenix, flour on the store shelf may contain only half the moisture that it would in Seattle, and therefore, I must compensate by adding more water to recipes. You may need less. Adjust accordingly to your own climate and make notes and substitutions in the recipes below. I suggest starting with only half the water listed, and adding more as necessary up to the amount mentioned. Aim for a soft, easily pliable but not mushy dough, sort of like pre-warmed and easy-to-mold Play-doh. If it feels stiff, it contains too little water.

I'll start here with an easy grain recipe, which can be made in as little as 20 minutes and provide a quick and healthy start to your day. At the end of this section is a longer but straightforward recipe for making your own bread. While bread may seem daunting, it is so basic to human existence that every cook should acquire this skill. Once you know how to make your own bread, you will wonder how you ever did without it.

# Quick Bread: Biscuits

If you're too hungry to wait for a more elaborate meal, here's a quick biscuit recipe that can have you eating biscuits in about 20 minutes.

Yield: 12 small or 8 large biscuits

Ingredients:
2 level cups of All Purpose Flour (plus a little extra for rolling)
1 rounded tablespoon of baking powder (do not mistakenly use baking soda)
1 level teaspoon salt
1 level teaspoon sugar, if desired (optional)
Up to 1 cup milk (depending upon the humidity in your geographical location) This could be regular, almond, soy, etc.
⅓ cup of organic vegetable shortening

Utensils needed:
measuring spoons
measuring cups
pan or cookie sheet

parchment paper

large spoon for mixing

regular oven or toaster oven

**1.** Pre-heat oven to 375 degrees. Heat a cup of milk for about 70 seconds in the microwave.

**2.** While the milk is heating, mix the dry ingredients together in a bowl. Spoon the shortening into the ⅓ measuring cup and press down, to make sure that there are no air pockets in the cup and it is completely filled with shortening. Afterward, spoon all of that shortening into the dry ingredients. Work the shortening through the flour mixture with your clean hands or a pastry cutter, so that it is evenly distributed throughout the mixture.

**3.** Add half a cup of milk to the flour mixture and stir. Continue to add the rest as needed to make a very soft dough that forms a single ball. (Make sure the dough is very soft and pliable, not much firmer than cream cheese.)

**4.** Cut the ball into 8 or 12 even pieces, depending upon if you want large or small biscuits. Flatten each piece slightly. Use extra flour if needed to keep the biscuits from sticking to your hands as you work with each.

**5.** Line a pan or cookie sheet (about 9"x15") with a sheet of parchment paper and place each biscuit on the parchment paper, evenly spaced. Bake them for about 15 minutes.

**Mom's common sense notation: In this or any other recipe, never substitute any other paper for parchment paper.**

**Caution:** Don't over bake, even for a few minutes. Biscuits in the oven for five minutes longer than necessary will probably be burned on the bottom. Experiment with the time, since all ovens are different. Try 12 minutes if the biscuits are too brown, or 17 if not done. Even two minutes makes a big difference.

**Biscuit option:** Cut a finished biscuit in half, top both halves with cheese, jalapeno and tomato, and microwave for 60 seconds for a hot, open-faced sandwich. Experiment with toppings to achieve different results. If you like a crusty sandwich, don't use a microwave. Place it in a toaster oven for 4 or 5 minutes at 375 degrees instead.

# Tortillas

While tortillas are a bit of a challenge for a novice, they are so prevalent in our Southwest culture that I felt I had to include them. Store-bought tortillas generally use preservatives and other undesirable ingredients; nothing beats fresh, hot tortillas straight off the griddle. You'll get the hang of these in no time.

Yield: 4 large or 8 regular tortillas. If you wrap them well so that absolutely no air gets in, they can be frozen and taken out as needed. If you are cooking only for yourself and want fresh tortillas, cut all ingredients in half to make 2 large tortillas.

Ingredients:
1 1/2 level cups of All Purpose Flour (plus a little extra for rolling)
3 tablespoons Grape Seed Oil (you may substitute coconut, olive or whatever cooking oil you have)
1/4 teaspoon of Baking Powder
1/2 teaspoon salt
Up to 3/4 cup hot water (depending upon your location)

Utensils needed:

Griddle or very large frying pan

Measuring spoons: teaspoon and half-teaspoon

Measuring cup

Large bowl

Mixing spoon

Wooden cutting board, large

Rolling Pin

Large Spatula (used for turning pancakes, etc)

Waxed paper or plastic wrap

**1.** Heat the water for 60 seconds in the microwave (or on the stove.)

**2.** While the water is heating, add the flour, salt and baking powder to the bowl and mix well.

**3.** Add the grape seed oil to the dry mixture. Pour it all in and spread evenly throughout the dough. Put your clean hands into the dough and break up the oil to make a crumbly, even textured mixture. This will take a minute or two to distribute the oil.

**4.** Add the hot water gradually while mixing the dough until it is all stuck together in one mass. Make sure that the dough is soft and pliable. Discard any excess water.

**5.** Pick up the dough and knead it for just a minute (kneading instructions are included in the bread recipe). Make sure that the dough is nice and soft but not too sticky. If it is hard to knead, it is too dry. If too sticky, add flour.

**6.** Put the dough back into the bowl and cover it with waxed paper or plastic wrap to keep it nice and moist. Turn your griddle to the highest setting and let it heat up for about 10 minutes. Do not use any oil on the griddle; it must remain dry to make good tortillas.

**7.** Generously coat a wooden cutting board with a tablespoon or so of flour (if you don't have enough flour on the cutting board, the dough will stick to it and you will have a mess on your hands.) If you don't have a large cutting board, use a clean section of countertop, sprinkled with flour.

**8.** Cut your dough into either 4 or 8 pieces, depending upon whether you want to make small tacos or large burritos. Roll each of the pieces in a ball and dust with flour. These balls should be really soft and easy to work with, but not watery or super sticky. Put them all back in the bowl and cover with plastic wrap or wax paper to keep the air out.

**9.** Take out the dough balls one at a time so that they don't dry out. Flatten the ball and place it on the floured board. Sprinkle flour on top and then start rolling the ball into a thin, round shape with the rolling pin. Work with the rolling pin in a north-south direction, then east-west, then northeast-southwest, then northwest-southeast. Keep flattening the tortilla out wider and wider. Don't worry about forming a perfect circle. I guarantee that unless you use a tortilla press, you will not get a perfectly round tortilla. It doesn't matter. All that matters is that it tastes good.

**10.** Once the tortilla is fairly flat, pick it up (taking care not to fold it over) and sprinkle more flour on the cutting board. Then place the tortilla on the cutting board again, this time with the other side turned up. Roll it again until the dough is very thin (the thickness of three sheets of paper or so.) When the tortilla hits the griddle, it will puff up and thicken.

**11.** Place the tortilla on the hot side of the griddle (the side closest to the heating element.) Save enough room for the second tortilla. Make sure the griddle is hot enough before you place your tortilla on it.

**12.** While you are waiting for the first one to cook, start rolling out your second one. Make sure to follow all the instructions for the first one, including flouring the board again. Cover the rest of the dough with plastic wrap again to avoid drying it out.

**13.** When you are through rolling out your second tortilla, the first one on the griddle will be ready to turn (about 90 seconds). Take a large spatula and flip the first tortilla to the opposite side of the griddle (the one away from the heating element.) It's already well formed and should not fall apart when you flip it. After you've done that, take the second tortilla and place it on the griddle in the spot that the first tortilla just vacated. If there is excess flour in that spot on the griddle, just brush it off with a spatula before placing the second tortilla. Afterward, roll out your third.

**14.** By the time you finish rolling the third tortilla, the first one should have light brown spots on the bottom. Take it off the griddle and cover it with a sheet of waxed paper or plastic wrap. (If the spots are too dark, cook the next tortilla for a minute less.)

**15.** Flip the second tortilla over to the far side of the griddle, away from the element, just as you did with the first one. Place your third tortilla in the vacant spot on the griddle, next to the heating element. Keep following the same routine for all of the tortillas. Once they are all done, turn off the griddle.

**TIP:** Don't let the tortillas dry out. They become brittle and crack if exposed to air. If you aren't going to use them within a couple of minutes, wrap them tightly and avoid all air pockets. If they do dry out and turn brittle, you may save them by sprinkling each tortilla with water and then microwaving it for 20 seconds. If that doesn't work, cover it with cheese and other toppings and stick in the oven for quesadillas!

**French Toast**

Yield: 3 pieces of toast

Ingredients:
3 slices of bread
1 egg
1/3 cup of milk
1/2 teaspoon of vanilla
1 teaspoon sugar
1 tablespoon oil (coconut, grape seed or other healthy oil)

Utensils needed:
Griddle
Spatula
Bowl
Fork or egg beater to stir the mixture

**1.** Brush griddle with oil and heat until hot on the highest setting.

**2.** Crack open your egg into a bowl. Add the milk, vanilla, and sugar. Stir mixture thoroughly. If desired, you may beat it with an egg beater for extra fluffiness.

**3.** Once the griddle is hot, dunk your bread into the egg mixture. Coat both sides of the bread and then arrange your slices on the griddle nearest the element.

**4.** Cook for approximately 90 seconds on each side, flipping them half-way through the cooking process. (If they stick to the griddle, they are not ready to flip.) Once they are nicely browned, remove from griddle and serve warm with syrup, jam or butter and sugar.

## Pancakes

Yield: about 5-6 pancakes
Ingredients:

1 cup of flour
1 cup of milk or almond milk (or less, depending upon your geographical location)
1 egg

1 teaspoon of sugar

1 teaspoon of baking powder

Pinch of salt (a tiny amount; see the measurements section)

½ teaspoon of vanilla flavoring

1 teaspoon plus 1 tablespoon oil (The teaspoon goes into
the batter, while the tablespoon greases the griddle.)

Utensils needed:

Griddle

Spatula

Large Bowl

small bowl

Large Spoon

Measuring cup and spoons

pastry brush

ladle

**1.** Turn on griddle and set to the highest setting. Brush 1
tablespoon of oil on the griddle using a pastry brush.

**2.** Mix the dry ingredients together in a large bowl and stir
to combine. (flour, sugar, baking powder and salt)

**3.** Pour one cup of milk into the small bowl. Add one egg, a
teaspoon of oil and a half teaspoon of vanilla. Stir the liquid

mixture together to blend, and then pour it into the dry ingredients.

**4.** Stir the batter thoroughly, making sure to scrape the bottom to incorporate the dry flour. If it is too thick, add a little more milk. (It should feel like a creamy milkshake.) If it's too thin, add flour. As soon as you have the consistency the way you like it, take a ladle full of batter and pour it onto the griddle. You may be able to fit 6 pancakes on the griddle at once, three on top and three on bottom, depending upon the size of the griddle. Remember that the middle part of the griddle is cooler than the outer edges. Food placed there will take longer to cook.

**5.** As soon as you see defined holes form over the tops of the pancakes, they are ready to turn over. The more holes you see on the top of the pancakes, the browner the other side will be. Use your spatula and flip the pancakes over to cook the other side for about 1-2 more minutes. As soon as both sides are browned, take the pancakes off the griddle.

VARIATION: Add one mashed banana, diced peeled apples, or other fruit to the batter and blend it well. You may also add a half teaspoon of cinnamon, if desired.

# Basic Bread

Baking bread is an ancient skill that is basic to human survival. Nowadays, so many people forego ever learning that precious talent, and yet home-baked breads are generally healthier and more satisfying because you've baked it yourself. It's one of the last recipes you should try, and yet once you've done it a few times, it will be a no-brainer to prepare.

Good bread takes time. It's not something you can do in the hour before school or work. From the time you start until you have the hot loaves rolling out of the oven, it will take about three hours. Don't let that daunt you, however, since most of the time is spent waiting for the loaves to rise or bake!

Before we dive into basic white bread, let's start with a few tips on flour and yeast:

## Tips on Flour

For those without sensitivity to regular flour, just look for "All Purpose" for general baking needs. This will be the kind you use most often. Frankly, I've never found a need for cake flour, but if I were a gourmet chef I suppose I would use it. Bread flour is useful but not nearly as much benefit as one might think, and it is generally more expensive. Buckwheat flour is useful for making your breads healthier and giving them a denser, darker look and texture. Don't make the mistake of using all buckwheat, however. There is no gluten in buckwheat, and without gluten, bread will not rise and you'll have a rock instead of a loaf. Use no more than one fourth to one third buckwheat (or other non-gluten flour) in any recipe that calls for flour.

**Tips on Yeast:**

Whenever possible, use instant dry yeast. Don't confuse "instant dry" with "double acting dry" yeast. They are not the same. The double acting comes in little packages or jars that are quite expensive. The kind of yeast I use is Saf Instant Dry. It comes in a one-pound, square plastic bag about 4" high. You can find it at Winco Foods for a few bucks, or online at amazon.com or vitacost.com (two of my favorite sites for food). While you use more of the instant dry than you would the double acting, it is still worth it because it comes out cheaper overall and your breads dependably rise, no matter what the season. With double acting, there is more likelihood of failure.

For anyone living in a warm climate, or those who purchase online from a Southern manufacturer, stock up on yeast in spring and put it in the freezer to use throughout the rest of the year. If you buy yeast in summer or fall, there is a chance that it sat in a hot van on the way to the store and some of the yeast was killed. Yeast is a live culture and it dies if it sits in a hot delivery truck.

Remember, never pour salt directly on yeast, or vice-versa. When you add ingredients, make sure you stir the yeast into the flour before adding salt, so that the flour acts as a barrier between the yeast and the salt. Yeast hates salt (but loves sugar). However, don't let that deter you from using salt. It's necessary to keep the bread or other baked goods fresh. Too little salt, and your bread will turn stale within a day or two. With enough salt, it lasts at least three days and possibly more.

### White Yeast Bread

Yield: 3 medium or 2 large loaves. Keep one loaf out and freeze the rest until needed. That way, you'll have to bake less often.

Ingredients:

6 cups All Purpose Flour (plus about a cup extra for use while kneading)

3 rounded tablespoons of instant dry yeast

2 level teaspoons salt

2 tablespoons of honey or sugar

3 cups (more or less) of warm water. The water must be warm but not hot. Yeast will die at temperatures above 115 degrees.

1 tablespoon oil for greasing the pans

Extra tablespoon or two of flour for the pans


Utensils needed:

Measuring spoons: tablespoon and teaspoon

Medium bowl

Measuring cup

Large Bowl

3 medium or 2 large bread pans

Pastry brush (the thing in the kitchen utensils drawer that looks like a small paintbrush)

Pan of water (short in height but wide to hold a couple inches of water.)

Cookie sheet or baking stone

Large mixing spoon

Oven Mitt

Wooden cutting board or other surface for kneading the dough

**1.** Measure the honey or sugar into a medium bowl and add three cups of water. (If you live in a non-desert environment, start with two and add more if needed.) Stir well to mix the honey. Heat the water-honey mixture in the microwave for no more than 40 seconds, or until warm but not hot. (about 100 degrees)

**2.** While you are waiting for the water to heat, mix all dry ingredients (yeast, flour and salt) into a large bowl. Stir well between additions to keep the yeast and salt from making direct contact.

**3.** Pour in the water-honey mixture into the dry ingredients and stir thoroughly until the mixture forms a single mass. If the dough feels dry, add more warm water until it holds together in a nice, soft ball of dough. Don't worry about getting it too moist, you can (and will) add more flour later, and it is far better too wet than too dry.

**4.** After it is thoroughly mixed, turn the dough onto a well-floured surface. (If you have no large cutting board, then you can use a flat stovetop or counter, provided they have been thoroughly cleaned and rinsed.)

**5.** Wash out your dough bowl right away, while the dough is on the cutting board. If you don't do it now, the mixture will turn into a concrete-like substance that will be difficult to wash. After you've washed and dried it thoroughly, oil the bowl and set it aside on the counter. (To oil it, add a teaspoon of oil and rub it all over until the whole inside is coated.) Get back to the dough as quickly as possible.

**6.** Set the timer for at least 8 minutes or as long as 10, for a softer bread. Sprinkle flour on the top of the dough, and then "knead" it. In kneading, you pick up the dough with both hands and turn it over, then push the dough down on the sides and top. Every time you pick up the dough, you should turn it a quarter turn before pushing it down again. You're basically trying to make sure that every part of it is squeezed together and blended with every other part. This is important, not only to blend the ingredients but to distribute the gluten, which makes the bread rise.

Add as much flour as you need to keep the dough from sticking, to remain soft and pliable. If it's hard to push down, then it's too stiff. In that case, keep kneading without adding more flour. It should eventually become pliable, but if it doesn't, oil your hands and let the oil distribute into the dough for more pliability.

**Alternative:** If you have a mixer with a dough hook (An attachment that looks like a hook), you can let the machine do the work of kneading. However, you'll have to halve the recipe (use half amounts of all ingredients mentioned) in order for it to do a good job. Don't try to knead the full amount of dough in one batch. You'll likely strain the motor and destroy the machine.

**7.** Once the dough is thoroughly kneaded, turn it into the oiled bowl. Put it in the oven, but DO NOT turn the oven on, even on "warm." It will kill the yeast. However, you can warm up the oven by turning on the light.* That will help the dough to rise. Be certain that the light bulb isn't touching the bowl. Set the timer for 60 minutes.

*The light switch for my oven is located on the top of the stove on the left hand side. If yours is in a different location, write it down here:

_____

**8.** Take out 2 large or 3 medium bread pans. (Mediums make a 1 lb loaf; the large pans make about a pound and a half.) Put a few drops of oil (olive, grape seed or other oil) in each of the pans and use a pastry brush to distribute the oil evenly throughout the bottom and sides of the pan. Wipe off any excess. After this is complete, place a level tablespoon of flour in each of the pans and then shake them, in order to coat the sides and bottom with flour. Any excess flour can be thrown on the cutting board, since you'll need more later. Set the three pans aside for later use and clean up the kitchen from the flour residue (there will be lots of flour residue, if you are like me!)

**NOTE**: Some people use sprays to coat the pans. Do not use these unless you can find an organic spray with a safe propellant. The ones that most people use may not be safe for your long-term health. Stick with the method I've outlined for a healthy bread.

**9.** When the timer beeps at the end of an hour, take out the dough. It should have doubled in bulk. Turn the dough onto a floured board and roll it into a nice, smooth log. Cut the log into three pieces (or two for large loaves.) Remember to cut the side pieces slightly larger than the middle piece. Your eyes play tricks on you and if you cut them into what you think are equal pieces, you will find that the middle one is always bigger. If you cut the sides a little bigger than the middle, they should turn out equal in the pans.

**10.** Roll each of the loaves into a nice, smooth loaf that fits the pan. Don't worry about losing the "rise" that you got from the first rising. When I first started cooking, I tried to keep it risen, and this was useless. It's actually better if you flatten it all out and let it rise again a second time. The bread will turn out better that way.

**11.** Place a short pan of warm water on the lowest rack in the oven (in the lowest position). Adjust the upper rack to fit just above this pan but not so high that the rising loaves will touch the ceiling of the oven. Place a cookie sheet or baking stone on this upper rack, with the loaf pans spread evenly on the stone or cookie sheet.

**Tip:** Make certain that you don't place the three loaves too close to each other. If you do, then the bread may fuse together while baking and you'll have a hard separating them. Place them at least an inch apart, and well below the top of the oven.

**12.** Once again, let the dough rise in the cold oven (with the light on for warmth) for between 45 minutes to 1 hour.

Afterward, just turn on the oven and set to 375 degrees, with the timer reset to 55 minutes.

**Note:** Although many people believe that you need to preheat the oven before putting in your bread, I find that step unnecessary. This is the easy way to do it, because you don't have to bother with touching the loaves again until they are done.

**13.** When the timer goes off after 55 minutes, grab a large, clean towel. Place it on the counter. Turn off the oven and open it. Let the heat escape for a moment before putting your hand in to take the bread out. (Make sure you have an oven mitt on!) Pull out the three loaves, one by one, and turn them over onto the towel. If the loaf sticks to the pan, slide a knife all the way around the loaf, at the edges of the pan, until the loaf slides out. (If it sticks, make sure you use more oil and flour next time to coat the pan before adding the dough.)

After all three loaves are out of the pans and onto the towel, wrap them to where no air is getting directly at the loaves. Leave them in the towel for a half hour. This will allow the loaves to cool without getting hard.

**14.** After a half hour or more, open your towel and take out your loaves. Place them in bread bags (large, food grade plastic bags). I like to "double bag" my bread for the freezer, so put each loaf into one bag with a twist tie, and then put it in another bag (with the twist tie facing down, toward the bottom of the second bag.) Twist tie again. Make sure all air is squeezed out of both bags before you tie them. Place two loaves in the freezer like that, and then just place the third loaf in one bag and leave it on the counter. (This method is only for short-term storage. If you need to keep the bread frozen for more than a week, wrap it a third time in freezer wrap.)

There! You've accomplished a real feat! How many young people can say they've mastered bread making? Don't try to slice the bread until it is cold, unless you can't wait. It's very hard to slice hot bread without making a big crumbly mess. Once it's cool, enjoy your bread and compare it to Mom's. You'll find yours isn't too bad!

**Variation: Specialty Breads**

In the above recipe, substitute up to two cups of buckwheat for white flour, in equal measures. Your bread will be brown and denser, but very tasty. Or, add a cup of uncooked oatmeal to the bread, or a half cup of sunflower seeds. Use your imagination!.

For a "Wonder Bread" type of loaf, substitute milk for half of the water. You'll have to heat the milk a little longer to warm it, since it's refrigerated. You may also try adding a raw egg to the dough, for a different texture.

**Mom's Own Grain Recipes**

_____

_____

_____

_____

_____

_____

_____

# Beverages

## Coffee

Most people nowadays have drip coffee machines, and you can read the directions on any can of coffee to brew with that process. I threw away my drip machine long ago in favor of the old fashioned stovetop percolator, for better flavor. This recipe is for perked rather than drip coffee.

Yield: 1 pot, percolated

Ingredients:
up to ½ cup Coffee Beans
Water
1 dash (very small amount) of salt

Utensils needed:
Percolator Coffee Pot
Coffee Grinder

**1.** Make sure you have all the parts of the coffee pot: pot with lid (with the round glass top on the lid attached), metal basket with lid, and long stem with spring. (The spring is critical; don't lose it.)

**2.** Place slightly less than ½ cup of coffee beans into a coffee grinder. By slightly less, I mean measure out a level half cup and then take out 10 or so beans. Turn on the coffee grinder and grind for about 15 seconds. Take the metal coffee basket and set it on the counter. With your finger over the hole in the center, pour the coffee from the grinder into the basket and shake to distribute evenly. (You can also plug the hole with something small, like a wadded up paper towel, but that's too much work for me.)

**3.** Look inside the coffee pot and you will see a round metal screw just below the spout. Fill the pot with water to just below the bottom of that screw.

**4.** Once the pot is filled with water, add a dash of salt to the water. Place the stem inside and put the spring on the stem, with the large side of the spring on top. Slide the basket onto that stem and put the basket lid on the basket. Then place the coffee pot lid on top and press down. The spring will cause the basket to bounce a little as you press the coffee pot lid down, this is normal. Make sure you attach the coffee pot lid securely; you'll hear a little "bump" as you press the lid down. (If the lid seems extremely loose, you might have forgotten the spring or placed it wrong side down.)

**5.** Place the coffee pot on the burner and set the heat for "number 6" on the stove, or medium high. This is about one-third of the way from medium setting to the high setting on most stoves. Set the timer for 19 minutes. Once the timer beeps, make sure you take the coffee pot off the heat IMMEDIATELY (within 15 seconds or so) or else your coffee will continue to perk. Serve coffee with milk and sugar, if desired.

### Lemonade

Yield: 2 quart pitcher of lemonade

Ingredients:

Water and ice cubes

1/3 cup organic Lemon Juice (Santa Cruz or other concentrated lemon juice).

Alternative to Lemon Juice from a bottle: 3 fresh lemons

Sugar to taste

Utensils needed:

Measuring cups

Pitcher

Long Spoon

**1.** Fill a pitcher ¾ full with water.

**2.** Pour 1/3 cup of lemon juice into the pitcher; add ½ cup or more of sugar, depending upon your preference.

**3.** Stir well, add ice and enjoy!

### Chocolate Frosty

For a quick frozen dessert drink, you'll need a blender, a banana, a cup of milk or almond milk, a level tablespoon of cocoa powder, a teaspoon or two of sugar (as much as you wish), and about 8 or 9 ice cubes.

Put all ingredients into the blender and blend very well for about a minute or so. Make sure all the ice is blended in. Pour and enjoy!

**TIP:** Substitute strawberries, peaches or other fruit for the bananas. Omit the chocolate, if you wish, as a change of pace. This makes a great drink for hot summers.

# Mom's Favorite Recipes:

_____

_____

_____

_____

_____

_____

_____

_____

# Chapter Two

## Cleaning

No one likes to clean, but there are ways to make the jobs go faster. Some of these can be pushed off, but many are critical to the proper running of a household. This list may not be complete, but at least it should prevent any major catastrophes from occurring.

I put in parentheses the frequency that a job *should* be done, in my opinion. That doesn't mean I always did it that frequently; it just means I always intended to do so. Sometimes life got in the way. Aim for those targets, and if it doesn't happen, well, at least you tried!

I hope these tips will be useful to you, and that you will wind up even better at household chores than I ever was. Good luck.

## Dishes

Frequency: Twice or more daily

**Doing dishes by hand:**

Whether you have a sink full of dishes or only a few, soaking them first will make washing a breeze. If you only have a few, you can put them all into hot water at once and soak for five minutes, then wash each one. With a large amount, such as after a party, follow this procedure:

Separate the dishes into groups: Plates and small bowls, glassware, silverware, and large serving pieces, pots and pans. Place the glassware group (cups and glasses) in the sink and add hot water, along with one big squirt of dish liquid (approximately a tablespoon if you were to measure it, but don't! Just squirt it into the sink.)

Fill the sink to about ¾ full with the hot, sudsy water. Let the glassware soak for about five minutes, or longer if the water is too hot for your hands (but don't wait for it to cool.) Take each piece out of the water and swish both inside and outside of the glassware with the dish scrubber (the long handled scrubbing tool with nylon bristles). Make sure the item is thoroughly clean and does not have any bits of food, lipstick marks, etc, on it. Rinse it in water (on the other side of a double sink, or if you don't have one, in a dishpan of water). Afterward, shake it dry and place in the dish drainer. Do the same with all items.

When the glassware is finished, add a little hot water to the sink to bring the water level back up to about ¾ full, and place the plates and small bowls in the water. While the plates are soaking, dry the glassware and put them away. By the time you're finished, the plates and bowls may be ready to wash. Take each plate and swish it with the dish scrubber or dishcloth until it's clean, rinse and then place in the drying rack. Once all of the plates and bowls are done, put the silverware into the soapy water.

Add hot water and if necessary, a little more dish liquid. While the silver is soaking, dry the plates and bowls and put them away. Afterward, follow the same procedure with the silverware.

The pots and pans will require longer soaking and really hot water, so drain some of the water and then run the tap until it is very hot again, adding more hot water to the sink. Place your pots into the water and let them soak for 10 minutes (or even an hour, if you want to go relax.)

Once the pots have soaked, take them out and scrub them. If the food is burnt on the pan, you may need some

Ajax or Comet cleanser to get them clean. Just sprinkle a bit of cleanser onto the burnt parts and use a sturdy scrub brush or scouring pad to scrape the pans clean. Make sure they are rinsed thoroughly afterward. Dry them and put them away, or leave them in the rack overnight, as I often do (when I'm lazy!) However, if you have cast iron pots (the best kind), don't let them air dry. Instead, dry them with a cloth. If you don't, they may develop rust.

**Doing dishes in a dishwasher:**

Scrape all the bits of food that you can off of the pots, pans and dishes before you put them into the dishwasher. Place the pots and really dirty items on the bottom rack. Glassware, plastic ware and delicate items go on top. Do not put any antiques, crystal stemware or carnival glass (that orange, iridescent glass from Grandma's day) into the dishwasher; wash those by hand. They're valuable!

Make sure the dirty part of each item is facing downward, toward where the jets of water will be most forceful. Add the recommended amount of dishwashing detergent into the cup that is made for detergent. **Never use**

**regular dishwashing liquid in a dishwasher** … you'll have a soapy mess all over the floor!

For added convenience (but extra expense) you may use those "gel packs" to avoid having to measure. Just toss an automatic dish detergent single gel pack into the cup meant for dish detergent and run the machine.

**TIP:** After washing and drying cast iron pans, add a teaspoon of olive oil to the pan, take a paper towel and coat the pan all over the inside and outside, to renew it. Make sure the pan is thoroughly dry before you begin this step.

### Laundry

Frequency: Once a week

Laundry is pretty simple, when you get the hang of it. I usually separate the items into three piles, but if there is little wash that week, two is sufficient. The light colored items go in one pile. The dark colored but not heavy items, such as shirts and dress pants, go in a second pile. The third pile is for heavy jeans, excessively tough items to clean, or sometimes, dirty towels. Anything that looks sturdy and tough can go into that pile.  Remember to wash anything newly bought separately, until you see if the color fades. Sometimes new things are not color fast, and can dye the rest of the wash.

Once you have separated the piles, open your washer and load the clothes. Try not to stuff the machine. Fill it about ¾ full and then add a quarter cup of laundry detergent. (Follow the detergent's directions for amount to add, but this is a general measure.) Some machines have a dispenser that you can add the liquid to. Others, you just pour it on the clothes. Make sure you pour it on a towel or unimportant item; it will mix with the rest of the clothes later. It is possible that the laundry detergent, if poured onto a piece of clothing that is not color fast, will cause the color to fade in that spot.

Turn the first dial to one of the following: "super load" "medium load" or "small load." A small load is less than half full (not pressed down). A medium load is between half but less than ¾ full. If you are in doubt, use the super load as that will get any sized load clean, but remember, it uses the most water. (Note: on most washing machines, you have to pull up the dial before you can turn it to the proper spot, and then push it down again.)

If the clothes are just "normally" dirty, or if you are washing thin or delicate items, turn the second dial to

"Permanent Press" at the 10 minute marker to start filling the machine with water. If there are jeans or a very heavy load, however, turn it to "Heavy Duty" at the 14 minute mark. Close the lid and let the machine do the rest of the work. (Note: Some machines will not start to fill up with water unless the lid is closed. Others work with the lid up, so you can check the load and add detergent, etc, to the water stream. However, never run a washer through its cycle with the lid up, even if it lets you.)

When the load is finished, take it from the washer to the dryer. Remove the lint filter in the dryer (that slot on the top or side of the dryer where you can pull out the mesh screen). Take out all of the lint and throw it away (unless you recycle lint for projects. Some people do.) Be very gentle with this screen; it can break.

Replace the lint filter back into the slot on the top of the dryer. Add one or two fabric softener dryer sheets if desired, depending upon if the load is large or small, then close the door and set the machine to between 50-70 minutes. Run until done. Remove clothes promptly and fold them, in order to avoid wrinkles.

While one load is in the dryer, you may run an additional load in the washer, so that you can do successive loads in the least amount of time. Since the washer does not take as long as the dryer, your washer load will finish long before the dryer load is done. Just leave it in the machine until the dryer is finished with the previous load, but don't accidentally forget a load in the washing machine. Make sure to dry it within a few hours of washing, or the clothes will "mildew," which means it will have spots on the clothes and smell bad.

**Tip: BE CAREFUL WITH BLEACH!**

Bleach can be used in order to disinfect clothes or get very stubborn stains out of white clothing. However, if you accidentally drip bleach on colored clothing, you will wind up with a stain that cannot be washed out. If your clothes get too yucky to wear, you can always put a quarter cup of bleach into a washing machine before you put any clothes in, then fill the washer to the water line in order to mix the bleach thoroughly with the water before adding any clothing. That will make your clothes brighter and may help with stains, but it will also cause your colors to fade a bit.

**Tip: Clothing Stains:**

Stains are very easy to get out of clothes if they are fresh. Once they are dried and set in, it may be very difficult to get them out. Although I do believe in DIY cleaning solutions, most of them take time and experience to learn. My suggestion to you, just starting out, is to buy a "stain pen," such as the "Tide to Go Instant Stain Remover." Then, if you get something like grape juice, salsa, or grease on clothing, you can just grab the stain pen and rub it over the spot. You don't have to change immediately that way. Try to clean the item as soon as possible, preferably that same day, or just soak it in the sink until you can do the laundry.

**IMPORTANT:** If you ever hear a loud thumping from your washing machine and it starts to shake like it's gone nuts, DO NOT call a repairman. It isn't broken. It just means your load is unbalanced. Open it, redistribute the load evenly, and voila! Your machine is fixed!

### Sweeping and Vacuuming

Frequency: Twice a week or after a spill.

Whenever sweeping or vacuuming, start with a clean broom or vacuum. Empty the dirt cup or clean the bottom of the broom bristles.

**Sweeping:** Sweep with wide strokes, paying attention to corners and under tables and other furniture. After you've swept all the dirt into one small pile on the floor, use the dustpan, which is the plastic tool in the broom closet that looks like a short-handled, wide shovel. Hold it at floor level with one hand and use the broom or brush in the other hand to sweep up all of the dirt. Take the dirt to the trash and then put the dustpan and broom back where they belong. Any small bits that remain on the floor can be picked up with a damp paper towel.

**Vacuuming:** As above, pay attention to corners and under furniture. When vacuuming, it's a good idea to run the vacuum hose under the cushions of the couch and behind the couch and chairs. Be careful not to vacuum up sharp or hard objects, as these could damage the vacuum. Anything large (bigger than a watermelon seed) should also be picked up separately to avoid clogging the machine. Once you are done, empty the vacuum cup.

**How to collect tiny items with your vacuum hose:**

If you've ever run a vacuum hose (the part you pull out to use by hand) over an area and sucked up a needle or a coin, you know that this can cause a problem for your vacuum motor. If you want to clean an area with a lot of little such items, just place a piece of sheer fabric, such as women's panty hose, over the vacuum hose. Secure it with a rubber band. When you run the vacuum over the area, the items will be sucked onto the panty hose but not beyond, so you can just pull off the tiny items into the waste basket.

## Washing Floors

Frequency, easy method: Once a week
Frequency, hard method: Once every 3-4 months

There are two ways to wash floors, the easy way and the hard way. The easy way is what you'll do most often, to get most of the grime off the floor. The hard way is when you super-clean the floor, to remove all the buildup in the corners, etc.

**Easy Way:**

Start with a newly-swept floor. Take a spray bottle of cleaner (any cleaner, such as pine sol or whatever) and "spot clean" (shoot a spray) on any big stains on the floor.

Go through the whole room (or house) and make sure you spot spray every stain.

Fill a bucket with hot water. (If you don't have a bucket and are using the sink, make sure there are no dishes nearby that the water can splash on, and clean the sink thoroughly after you are done.) Add your floor cleaner, such as ½ cup of Pine Sol or ¼ cup of concentrated orange oil. Take your mop, dip it into the water several times and then squeeze it out using the squeezing mechanism attached to the mop, if it has one, or your hands if it doesn't. Go over the floor, mopping the area well.

Every so often, dip your mop back in the bucket and swish it around, then squeeze it out again. This will help in two ways, firstly because the mop gets dirty and needs to be refreshed with soapy water. Also, it will dry out as it is used and become difficult to glide over the floor. Plan to do about 20 square feet of floor for every dip into the bucket. (I do not mean a 20x20 room, but rather, 20 individual square feet. If you have a very slick floor, such as linoleum, you may get by with less frequent dips in the bucket.)

Once you are all done, drain the water from the bucket and rinse out the mop. You should not walk on the floor until it is dry, which may take a few minutes to an hour, depending on the floor type.

**Mom's Cheat:** If you put on absolutely clean white socks, fresh from the laundry, you can walk on the floor before it's dry without leaving dirt marks.

**Hard Way:**

Start with a newly-swept floor. Get a bucket and fill it half-way with water. Add ½ cup of orange oil or pine sol. Take a scrub brush, a scraper (a plastic ice scraper works, but you must be careful not to scratch the floor) and a large, clean rag. Start on one corner of the floor and dip the scrub brush into the bucket, then scrub the floor on your hands and knees, making sure to get the corners where dirt builds up.

After you've scrubbed a section within arm's reach, take the cloth and wipe the area semi dry, picking up all the bits of debris from the corners and pushing them aside into a pile that will be discarded later.

Keep working your way across the floor, scrubbing and wiping. Your pile of debris will likely get larger as you keep pushing it aside into one pile as you work. If you find any stubborn, stuck-on debris, use your scraper to work it loose and then scrub over it and wipe.

Once you've reached the end of the room, pick up all the debris and throw it away. Dump the bucket of water outside (it will be really filthy, so don't dump it in the sink unless you have no other choice.) Use the hose outside to rinse out the bucket.

**TIP:** Take on only one room at a time when using the hard method, not the whole house. You'll be on your hands and knees almost the entire time, and the job will be extremely tiring. Schedule your rooms throughout the year so that you can avoid exhaustion.

### Cleaning Bathrooms

Frequency: Once or twice a week, depending upon how dirty it gets.

Items needed for cleaning:

Spray bottle of Pine Sol or Orange oil, or mom's special cleaner (see below)
Glass cleaner or vinegar
Kitchen cleanser, such as Ajax or Comet
Scrub Brush

Clean cloths (Use rags or old dish towels that will NOT be used for dishes any longer. Paper towels are very good.) Toilet Bowl Brush (in holder behind toilet)

We'll handle each job separately, to explain it thoroughly. One thing you must remember, however, is NOT TO MIX various commercial cleaning products without first making certain that they are safe when used together. Many cleaning products give off toxic fumes when combined, and may be very dangerous to breathe. Use only one product at a time and then rinse thoroughly, removing all traces of that cleaner, before using another type of cleaner on the same spot.

**Important tip!** Use all cleaners in a well ventilated room. Some of the cleaners may cause irritation if the room is not ventilated. Either open a window or turn on the exhaust fan.

Before you start, have a spray bottle filled with cleaning solution. Either use a commercial solution or make Mom's special cleaner, which is half vinegar and half Dawn dish soap (full strength, original blue). This will work for most things except glass (mirrors, etc.).

**Tub:** First, spray your cleaner on the tub "ring," that layer of dirt buildup on the sides of the tub. Leave the tub for 10 minutes, to soak that in. Once you come back, scrub that ring with a scrub brush. Then, close the stopper on the tub and add about a gallon of water to the tub.

Wipe the areas previously scrubbed with a cloth, and once the water mixes with the cleaner from the scrubbed areas, dip the cloth in the water and use that soapy water to clean the other parts of the tub, including the rim, the fixtures, etc. The cloth, once fully soaked with the soapy water, will clean everything fairly well. After you are done, drain the water from the tub and rinse the tub, or just use a dry cloth to dry it.

**Commode:** Add toilet bowl cleaner, or a spoonful of pine sol or orange oil inside the toilet. Use the white toilet brush (the one that sits in a plastic holder next to the commode) to scrub the inside of it. Once that's done, flush the toilet. To clean the outside of the commode, spray it with the cleaning spray and wipe it down with a disposable paper towel. Clean the top of the commode the same way, as well as the lid, with a fresh paper towel. Make sure you clean under the lid, top and bottom, and the rim around the toilet, which always gets dirty.

**Be careful with toilet bowl cleaner. It's one of the harsher chemicals and must be handled gingerly!**

**Shower:** For bathrooms with free standing showers, Spray the walls, faucets, shower head inside of the shower with cleaning spray. Wipe it down with a damp cloth. Use Ajax or Comet to scrub the floor of the shower, paying attention to the drain area and the corners. Wipe it with a damp cloth. Clean both the outside and inside doors of the shower with glass spray and wipe with a paper towel or soft cloth. If the shower has curtains rather than a door, check the bottom of the curtain for mold. Clean and thoroughly dry the curtain at least once a week, to avoid mold due to moisture.

**Tip: How to clean a crusty shower head**

If your shower head is encrusted with hard, scaly patches and doesn't spray out water jets very well, you can clean it by filling a plastic bag with a solution of 3 parts of vinegar and 1 part of dawn dish soap. swish it around to mix thoroughly, then carefully tie the plastic bag around the shower head using strong rubber bands to secure the bag. Make sure the cleaning solution reaches all parts of the shower head. In the morning, remove the bag and wash off the shower head. It will be like new.

**Sink:** Wet the sink, and then sprinkle Ajax or Comet over it. Use a clean damp cloth to scrub the sink, paying attention to the drain where dirt builds up as well as to any ring around the sink. Dampen the cloth again and let water drip from the cloth to the faucet area, then sprinkle a little cleanser on that area. Scrub it with the cloth, then rinse the cloth and wipe down the entire sink.

**Tip:** For sparkling faucets, clean them first, then wipe them with rubbing alcohol or even a little cologne, if you're out of alcohol.

**Floor:** Although floors are covered in another section, I just want to remind you that you should make sure to get that small strip of floor behind the toilet and around the bottom of the toilet. That part always gets dirty, and don't forget to wipe off the baseboards while you're at it.

**Mirrors:** The last thing you want to do in any bathroom is the mirrors, since if water splashes on them, it will ruin any cleaning job. Spray window cleaner on the mirror and then wipe with paper towels, starting first at the bottom and working your way up. The reason you start at the bottom is because the drips are working their way down, and you don't want the cleaner to dribble all over the bottom of the mirror frame.

**For stubborn stains on any bathroom fixture:**
**Method 1:** Use a cleanser such as Ajax or Comet. Sprinkle some directly on the stains and scrub immediately, then rinse.
**Method 2:** Pour full strength Dawn dish liquid (original blue) directly on the stain and leave for at least an hour, or overnight. Rinse the Dawn off and then scrub it with a scrubber, rinsing thoroughly.

## Dusting

Frequency: Once or Twice a Week

Dusting is probably the easiest job of all, but one that most people won't notice unless you let it go for too long. Plan to dust right before sweeping or vacuuming, so that any dust that fell to the floor will be swept away. Start with the highest objects. Use the large, fluffy dusting wand for wiping off the blades of the ceiling fans. These are a major dust trap. Next, dust the light fixtures. Dust only when the lights are off and cool; do not dust hot light bulbs. Once those are done, dust the picture frames, paying attention to the tops and bottoms where dust collects. The tops of door frames are also major dust collectors. Once you have these high areas, you can dust the furniture (television, book cases, tables, etc.) Use an ostrich feather duster for the lower objects, if you prefer, or you can use the large dusting wand anywhere it is convenient.

If you would like a shine when you dust, you can spray the duster with Scott's liquid gold or any other furniture polish. If you have many items or little knickknacks on a table, don't spray around them because it will only cause a mottled effect, with some shiny parts and some dull. If you have a flat, empty surface, you may spray it directly and then wipe it with a clean cloth. Sprays are optional; plain old dusting is just fine.

### Refrigerator

Frequency: Every one to two weeks

Cleaning out the fridge is not that difficult, and it is a good idea to do it every week. I just never found the time, and so I often pushed it off to two weeks. Of course, if you do that, make sure you check every few days for spoiled food and throw it away. You don't want to leave rotten food for two whole weeks.

If you haven't cleaned out the fridge in a while, make sure to take all the food out of it; every bit, and put it on the counters. This makes it so much easier than if you clean shelf by shelf. After all the food is out of the fridge, spray all of the shelves, the sides and back of the fridge with a spray cleaner. Turn off the fridge while you work; there's a dial on the inside of the fridge, usually near the top. Turn that to "zero." On some refrigerators, you must turn off both the freezer and fridge, rather than just one. Whatever you do, don't forget to turn it back on again when you're done cleaning!

You can use a commercial cleaner like 409, or you can make your own with a spray bottle filled with water and a ½ cup of orange oil. If you don't have a spray bottle, just use a bowl of the cleaning mixture and dip your rag into it. Let the shelves soak in cleaning solution, then wipe it away. Use a scraper if anything is stuck onto the shelves. If you have wire shelving, use a soft scrub brush on the shelves. After you have wiped it all down, rinse your rag with clean water and wipe everything down again. Clean the door shelves thoroughly, getting all the corners that trap food.

The big plastic bin, the one that holds fruits and veggies, should be pulled out and washed. Take all the fruits and veggies out and then fill the bin with warm water and ¼ cup of orange oil or pine sol. Let it sit for a few minutes if it has dried bits that need to work loose. Once it's clean, rinse it out and then dry it thoroughly before you put any food back in, so that moisture doesn't cause fruits and veggies to rot prematurely.

**TIP:** I like to line the bottom of the veggie bin with paper towels, just to help keep moisture down.

After the inside of the fridge is all clean, put your food back into it. I usually add the fruits and veggies to the bin first, (check for bad spots and bruises as you go) and then put the milk cartons into the door. Items that you use every day should be placed in the most convenient spots. Throw away anything that's old.

The freezer is not cleaned as often as the fridge, because it doesn't get as dirty. When you clean it, follow the example for the fridge. When you put the food back, check for "freezer burn." It makes the food look a funny, washed-out color. That usually happens when food is not properly wrapped or too old. Throw out anything that doesn't look right.

Once you are through with the inside, clean the outside of the fridge and get the top of it, where dust collects. I don't do this near enough, but try to hit it at least every couple months, because the dust really builds up. You can use the dusting wand on the back of the fridge, to clean the coils, every few months. Also, the grill at the bottom of the fridge needs to be cleaned every couple months, and the water filter needs to be replaced every 3 months. Check the filter box for instructions. If you don't have a replacement filter, go online and check the fridge make and model (inside the door) for the proper filters.

When you turn the freezer/fridge back on, set it about half way between the "colder" and "coldest" setting. In a few hours, check to see if anything in the fridge is getting frosty. If so, you can lower the fridge setting. If items in the freezer are not yet frozen, set it to a colder setting.

## Washing Windows

Washing windows is luckily a job you don't have to do every week, or even every month if you are particularly busy. The main thing to remember when washing windows is to prevent streaks by washing them in the shade, when the sun is not facing the window. That way, you'll be able to see if there are streaks, and remove them.

Use crumpled newspapers, paper towels, or any lint-free cloth to wash windows. You can either use a commercial window spray, like Windex, or get an empty spray bottle and fill it with 2 cups of water and a half a cup of vinegar. Shake well. If the windows are really dirty and yucky, add half a teaspoon of dish liquid to the mix.

While you're at it, you can squirt some into the window track and clean that out too, but just be careful not to use the same cloth to wash the windows afterward. It will be filthy; the window tracks (where the windows slide) always get clogged with dirt.

After you wash the windows, dry them with a lint-free cloth or just use a squeegee, as you would use on your car window, in order to remove all the drips. Once there are no spots dripping, you can let them air dry.

# Cleaning the Oven

Most ovens are so easy now, because they are "self-cleaning." However, I will describe both types of cleaning, just in case you are ever without a self-cleaning oven.

## Self Clean Method:

Make certain that everything is out of the oven that could possibly melt, including silicone mats that can't take high heat. I sometimes leave my cast iron pot in the oven while I self-clean, just so that it will get clean too, but this is up to you. (It had better be a very good pot; the cheap ones won't cut it. Also, make sure it doesn't have a plastic or silicone handle. It must be all metal.) Check the drawer underneath the oven and make sure there is nothing in there that might melt. Once you've checked the oven for anything meltable, then just close the oven door, set it to "clean" and let it do its thing for the next few hours. You won't be able to open the oven door until it's finished, so don't clean the oven if you are going to need it within a few hours.

After the cycle ends (3 or 4 hours) wait until the oven is cool and then open it. You will see a fine ash covering the walls and the bottom of the oven. Use damp paper towels to remove this ash from the top, bottom and sides of the oven as well as the inside of the oven door. You'll need quite a few paper towels, because they will get black quickly. Don't use a cloth towel unless you're willing to bleach it thoroughly before using for anything else. Once the oven is wiped out, you're ready to bake again.

**Non-Self Clean Method:**

If you don't have a self-cleaning oven, then take everything out as mentioned before, and start with an empty oven. Take out the racks too, so that it will be easier to clean. Heat the oven to 250 degrees and set the timer for 10 minutes. When the timer beeps, put on rubber gloves and a face mask, if you have it (oven cleaner is nasty; thank goodness for self-cleaning ovens!). Once you have those on, take your spray oven cleaner (any brand will do) and spray the stuff on the top, bottom and sides of stove. Make sure the spray gets everywhere to clean it thoroughly, and then close the door and wait until the oven is cold enough to clean (about a half hour).

When the oven is cool to your hands, put on your face mask and gloves and get a damp rag or sponge and clean off all of the spray foam from the top, bottom and sides of oven. Make sure you get it ALL, because if you don't, that horrible chemical can get in your baked food. Once you've cleaned it all off, then take a wet rag and rinse everything well. Clean the racks with soapy water and put them back in the oven.

**Tip:** Use oven cleaner in a WELL VENTILATED space. Open a window before you start. Believe me, you'll need it!

## Ironing

Ironing is a job I almost never have to do anymore. When I was younger, it was a weekly chore, but now, I do it every few months. All of my clothes are permanent press, so I no longer have huge, deep wrinkles in clothing.

If for some reason you need to iron something because it wrinkled, make sure you use the lowest setting that will get the job done. If it's too high for the fabric type, it will burn the cloth. Always dampen the item you are ironing, or if you have a steam iron, fill it with water. To do this, stand your iron on end and fill the little hole at the top with distilled bottled water (tap water is usually too hard for the iron). It may take a quarter-cup of water to fill.

Once the iron is full of water, turn it on and let it heat. When it's hot, you can iron the item, first flattening it out on the ironing board and then using short strokes to iron. Don't try to iron more than one layer of fabric at once; you'll likely create wrinkles that are worse than the wrinkles that you are trying to fix, so be careful.

### General Cleanup

For general cleaning of counters, tables, etc, use a mild detergent. I like to take a clean rag and dip it into the water after I've done the dishes, while the water is still hot. Squeeze it out and run it over the sink, counters, stove, etc. Make sure you clean the sink out after you do the dishes, because bits of food at the bottom can harden and, over time, can "pit" the sink with little marks.

You can make a stronger cleaning solution by filling a bucket half full with hot water and pouring in a cup of Pine Sol or a ½ cup of orange oil concentrate. This is useful for cleaning the tops of baseboards, dirty walls and doors, etc.

Make sure you clean the kitchen counters every day and after every main use, because that is the area where people place food. It's important for that area to be clean.

Clean the table and wipe it down daily as well, or after every meal.

**Tip:** Disinfect your wooden cutting board with salt. After you've cleaned and dried it, sprinkle salt on the surface and rub it in. Afterward, season your cutting board with a tablespoon of oil rubbed over both sides of the board. Use paper towels to rub the oil in and rub off any traces of salt. Remember, if you don't season your cutting board with oil at least once a month, it will eventually warp or split.

**Minimal List of Cleaning Supplies to have on hand:**

**Consumable items** (things you will buy again and again)
Ajax or Comet Cleanser, or a generic brand
Dawn Dish Liquid
Vinegar or window cleaner
Paper Towels
Bleach
Laundry Detergent
Fabric Softener (the dryer sheets are the best for no-mess softening)
If desired, you may add:
commercial all purpose cleaner, such as 409

**Non-Consumable Supplies needed:**

If you are setting up a household, you will need these minimum cleaning basics:

Broom and dustpan

Mop and bucket

Cleaning scrub brush

Assorted cleaning rags

Duster, such as an ostrich feather duster or a dusting wand.

Dishwashing bottle brush

Dishwashing pot scrubber

Toilet brush with holder

Buy a vacuum cleaner as soon as possible. Canister vacuums get into tight spots, but they are less convenient, as a rule, than uprights. Lugging a canister behind you can get to be a pain. I recommend a lightweight, upright vacuum.

# More Cleaning Tips from Mom:

_____

_____

_____

_____

_____

_____

_____

_____

# Chapter Three

## Shopping, Bills, Budgeting

Since shopping is usually done every week, we'll start this chapter with shopping and end with the monthly bill paying and budgeting. There are many items that make up a shopping list. The following supply list includes what I consider the "must haves," which you must have on hand each week. For those who eat meat, this list will be different than for ovo-lacto vegetarians like us.

There are also many "nice to have" items that usually find their way into my shopping basket, but if we have to live without them, we can. I've not included those here, but you might wish to add such things as specialty desserts, snacks, or exotic fruits.

## Pantry Supplies

Try to keep the following items on hand for any of the recipes in this book, or just for general use.

140

Flour

Sugar, honey or other sweetener

Salt

Herbs or Spices

Olive, Coconut or other Oil

Peanut Butter

Cereals

Oatmeal or other hot grain cereal

Baking powder

Spaghetti or other pasta

Spaghetti sauce

Coffee, cocoa or tea

Nuts, assorted (a great snack if you've had a hard day)

Maple syrup

Canned soup or chili (for days when you can't cook)

Yeast (If you're going to bake, you should have yeast. I use Saf Instant Dry Yeast)

Other snacks as desired

Rice

Bread and crackers

Water or other drinks

Other Supplies you might need for the pantry:

_____

_____

_____

_____

_____

_____

**NOTE:** The shelf life of items varies. You can keep commercial bread for up to a week, while things like sugar and salt will outlast your lifetime, as long as they remain dry and sealed. Check this link for the shelf life of different items, and remember, they err on the side of caution, so you may be able to use some items longer:

**http://food.unl.edu/food-storage-chart-cupboardpantry-refrigerator-and-freezer**

# Fridge Supplies

Butter (Use margarine only if you can't get butter, since
new studies show that butter is healthier than margarine.)
Milk or Almond Milk and any other dairy product
Eggs
Cheese
Veggies (celery, lettuce, tomatoes, cucumbers, carrots,
potatoes, zucchini, bell peppers, hot peppers, onions, etc.)
Fruits (apples, bananas, pears, peaches, plums, berries, etc.)
Condiments (mustard, catsup, or other condiments)
Tortillas (if you don't wish to make them, buy a good
commercial brand)

**Note:** Although many people think that you shouldn't put
bananas in the fridge, yes, you should, but only after they
are ripe. If you put them in before they're ripe, they'll
never get soft and delicious. However, if you put them in at
their peak, they will stay good for at least an extra 5 days.
The outside will turn dark, that's true, but the inside will be
perfectly fresh and firm!

**Freezer Items:**

Most freezer items are optional, but it's useful to have frozen veggies on hand, along with ice cream or sherbet, and of course, ice cubes for drinks. If you think you won't use bread before it gets too old, freeze it (properly wrapped). It will keep for weeks in the freezer.

**TIP:** How to Wrap Freezer Items: Food that goes into the freezer must be carefully wrapped in order to avoid "freezer burn," which causes food to dry out and change its texture in a short period of time. Once that happens, the food is virtually inedible. If you are only going to freeze an item for a few days, you can get away with double wrapping it in plastic bags. With this method, just put the food in a food-grade plastic bag, push all the air out of the bag and then tie it with a twist tie. Afterward, place the bag in another plastic bag with the twist tie down (toward the bottom of the bag) then repeat by sucking out all the air and tying it with a second twist tie.

If you want to store the food for longer than a few days, this method will not avoid freezer burn. For longer storage, use freezer wrap. It's in the "foils and wraps" section of the supermarket and comes in a roll. It looks like regular white paper on one side with a plastic coating on the other. First, wrap your food carefully in plastic wrap or waxed paper, leaving no air bubbles, and then wrap generously with freezer wrap, taking out as much air as possible, and then taping it shut.

**Shopping tip:** Don't underestimate the value of parchment paper in baking pizza, cookies, or anything that needs to retain crispness without burning. For years, I avoided parchment paper as an unnecessary expense. In my later years, I've learned that it helps to avoid burning the bottoms of crusts. If you're going to bake, make sure you have a roll of parchment paper on hand.

**Health tip:** Don't wrap food directly in aluminum foil. The food will absorb some of the aluminum, which may be bad for your health. You can read an article on it here: http://saveourbones.com/stop-doing-this-with-aluminum-foil/ Do not use foil pans to bake or cook with, either, unless you line it carefully with parchment paper first. If you want to wrap food that is still warm, wrap the food with a sheet of waxed paper or plastic wrap first, and then use the foil.

## Picking and Storing Produce

Choose produce that is free of blemishes. Glide your fingers over fruits to see if there are any softer spots. Your produce should be free of such spoilage. After you get home with your items, make sure you wash and dry them thoroughly to avoid mold, and then place them in your vegetable bin in the fridge. You can sort them in plastic bags to keep them neat, if desired, provided you dry them and then put a scrap of paper towel in the bag to absorb any trace of moisture.

Whenever possible, choose organic produce. This is particularly important for soft or thin-skinned items such as peppers, tomatoes, apples, pears, etc. While thick-skinned items, such as watermelon, will retain fewer pesticides than thin-skinned produce, there may still be enough to cause harm to human health. Therefore, spend the extra money and get organic if you can possibly manage to do so.

All certified organic produce (with the USDA certified label) is currently also Non-GMO. GMOs, or genetically modified organisms, may cause health risks. Look for either the "Certified Non-GMO" or the "USDA

Certified Organic" label on all food items purchased. (This includes produce and any other packaged items.)

## Finding Bargains

Most major grocery stores have a website where you can check this week's specials. Google the name of two or three stores nearest you and check their specials before heading to the store. Stock up on your favorite foods that are on sale this week, so you won't have to pay more next week.

Create a meals list for the week. Decide what you will probably eat and then purchase the items you'll need to create those dishes. After you've done that, you'll have a good idea what you want to purchase from the store and will not overspend.

Check out sites like Amazon.com and Vitacost.com to purchase non-perishable groceries online. They sometimes have better bargains than the local stores, and carry a full line of organic food. With free shipping on many orders, you can stock up on the things you need.

**Definition:** "Perishable food" is any food that spoils

quickly and usually requires refrigeration or freezing. "Non-perishable food" is food that you can leave on the pantry shelf and that lasts for at least a few weeks or longer.

### Miscellaneous Purchases

In addition to the cleaning supplies mentioned earlier, you will need some non-food items at the grocer or discount store. Plan on stocking these as soon as possible:

Plastic wrap, waxed paper and foil
(less frequently) parchment paper and freezer paper
bathroom tissue
large black trash bags
smaller white kitchen trash bags
coffee filters, if needed for coffee maker
paper towels
storage containers
light bulbs (have on hand in case one goes out)
flashlight and batteries
basic hand tools kit (wrench, 2 types of screwdrivers, etc.)
rolls of tape (adhesive, duct, and electrical tape for small repairs)

# Your Very First Shopping List

While the above items are handy to have all the time, there are some products that can wait for later. If you're away from home for the first time and have brought nothing with you but your clothes, the following lists will tell you what to purchase IMMEDIATELY. The first section lists grocery items if you are living in a completely furnished apartment, dorm or rooming situation, with linens and kitchen utensils, but no meals or maid service.

The additional items at the bottom include those things required if you have just rented an unfurnished studio and are staring at four empty walls and a suitcase full of clothes. If you are in a situation halfway between the two, then just pick and choose whatever you need from the list.

This will get you through the first few days of residency. As you acclimate yourself to your situation, you will search for furnishings and tools that make life more pleasant. For now, however, you'll survive with only the following items:

**Grocery Store:**
Food:

3 or 4 lbs of fruits and veggies, assorted (apples, pears, bananas, tomatoes, cucumbers, lettuce, bell peppers, zucchini, or other veggies or fruits)

1 half gallon of milk or almond milk

a package of cheese (or meat, if you eat it)

a half dozen eggs

a loaf of bread

a box of cereal

a couple cans of soup

a couple cans of chili

coffee, tea, juice, soda or other beverages

1 bag of sugar

1 container of salt

a package of nuts or other snacks

1 bottle of olive oil

1 jar of peanut butter

a package of spaghetti or other pasta

a jar of spaghetti sauce

a package of tortillas

a couple of frozen packaged meals, if desired

Non-Food:

1 spray bottle of all purpose cleaner

1 bottle of dish detergent

1 bottle or box of laundry detergent

packaged bar soap, such as Ivory soap

1 package of paper towels

1 package of bathroom tissue

1 box of kitchen trash bags (white, 13 gallon, small and easy to dispose of)

1 box of plastic wrap

1 box of aluminum foil

1 stick of deodorant

1 tube of toothpaste

1 bottle of shampoo

1 bag of disposable razors, if needed

1 bottle of multi-vitamins

1 tube of sunscreen

In case of illness or injury, make sure you purchase the following items right away (after all, you won't want to go to the store to get the items needed to feel well enough to go to the store!):

1 box of adhesive bandages, such as Band-Aids

1 bottle of Pepto Bismol or generic product (for stomach ailments)

1 bottle of acetaminophen or other pain killer

A pair of tweezers (for slivers)

1 box of cold and flu medicine, such as Theraflu

1 bag of cough drops

Lastly, in case you have rips in clothing or other items that need immediate attention, purchase a small "travel type" sewing kit. See instructions under the sewing section.

## Additional items:

If you are in an empty apartment without any furnishings or even household items, make sure you have:

a camp cot, a good sleeping bag or linens and blankets (at least 2 sets of sheets, plus blankets)
a folding table and folding chair set (You can get both this and the camp cot from a camping store or a large discount store such as Wal-Mart. This will actually prove useful later, either for camping or as an additional cheap table to use as a laptop desk, stand for a lightweight TV, etc.)
2 bath towels and 2 washcloths
a box of plastic forks and spoons
paper plates and plastic or paper cups
1 decent all-purpose cooking pan with lid
1 metal or wooden spoon, large
1 spatula

1 decent paring/slicing knife

can opener, manual

bottle opener

colander/strainer

oven mitt

flashlight and batteries, in case the power goes out


If the apartment does not provide a shower curtain or a bath rug set, you would be wise to get those right away. Also, make sure you have cleaning rags and a couple of dish towels, in addition to the roll of paper towels.

Almost anyone can survive the first few days with the above items, no matter what happens. You'll soon figure out what extra items you need to purchase and what you can do without.

### Paying Bills and Budgeting

Certain items will be paid monthly, such as rent, utilities, etc. Other items will need semi-annual or annual payments. Setting up "Bill Pay" with your bank's online website is the easiest way to pay ongoing bills. Set aside a regular day in which you pay bills. That will make it easer to remember. Although you may not have all of the following expenses, (or may have other additional expenditures) the following items might need to be budgeted:

Rent

Electricity or Gas/Propane

Water and Trash

Internet Service

Cable Television

Telephone/Cell service

Insurance (health, car, life, dental, etc.)

Car license and registration

Car, bank or loan payments

Student loans

Monthly bus passes

Groceries, both food and non-food

Medical bills

Clothing costs (purchases, dry cleaning, etc.)

Donations and gift purchases

Figure out your income and fixed expenses, so that you will know how much you have left over for flexible expenses. Keep track of receipts for expenditures such as donations, so that you can use them at the end of the year for tax purposes.

**Tip:** Check your bank balance at least every two weeks. If an unauthorized charge appears, notify your bank immediately. This is more common than you think, so stay on top of your checking account.

**Tip:** When purchasing checks for the first time, it's probably best to use the bank's service. However, when reordering checks, you may wish to utilize reordering services such as Current. They may save you money over the bank's check prices, and you can get different designs unavailable from your bank.

**Tip:** When purchasing health insurance, make sure you check the deductibles and co-pays. A deductible is the amount that you will pay per year before the insurance will START to pay anything. A co-pay is the part of the bill that you will pay after you have met your deductible. Sometimes, even if the cost of health insurance is a few dollars less per month, it is actually more expensive than another plan, if the deductibles and co-pays are high.

**Tip on car insurance:** Be certain to ask for all the discounts that you are entitled to, such as a non-smoker's discount, student discount, or safe driver discount. Talk to the agent to make sure you're getting everything to lower the premium. Also, it's often better to have a high deductible on car insurance, but check to see how much you'll pay by increasing the deductible. If it's more than a few dollars a month difference, go with the cheaper cost per month.

### Taxes

If you have only income taxes from a job and no self-employment income (such as from a farm or your own business), then doing your taxes by yourself is a snap. If you qualify to use a 1040EZ, that is by far the easiest one you can fill out. It's only one piece of paper. To see if you qualify to use it, go to IRS.gov and look up the instructions for 1040EZ.

If you have farm or business income, you'll have to fill out a regular form 1040 along with a Schedule C and a Schedule SE. If you aren't comfortable with it, you can go to the IRS office and ask their volunteers to help you fill it out. Please note, however, that the volunteers are not experts and may make errors. They will also not find all the deductions that can save you money. Going to a tax preparer such as H&R Block may get you extra deductions, but they charge a very hefty fee to find those, and there may be none to find.

The cheapest way to do your taxes is to follow the instructions and do them yourself. Go to IRS.GOV and download the 1040 instructional booklet, which contains many pages and explanations of the forms you will likely need. Afterward, go back to the site and print out those particular forms. If you only earned an income from one employer, you may only need the 1040EZ. If it's more detailed, I'm sure you'll get the hang of it if you try. You can always go to an IRS office after you've filled in the forms in order to have it reviewed by one of their volunteers before submitting it. Check when the volunteers are available, and if possible, make an appointment. Bring your proofs of deductions and expenses with you.

**TIP:** Plan to spend from half hour to two hours on your tax returns, depending on whether or not you have a small business. If it takes longer than that, seek professional help.

Remember that you need to do at least TWO tax returns, one for the federal government and one for your home state. Always do the federal form FIRST, since the state form often relies on the numbers you've calculated from the federal to determine your state taxes.

In order to do your taxes, you will need the following information and forms. If you earned a substantial income and qualify for itemized deductions, then do some research or hire a tax consultant. I'm going to assume that you are not Rockefeller or Trump, and only have a normal job from a normal company, or a small business or farm. When you start to earn a substantial income, seek professional help.

**You will need, at minimum:**

**1.** Your W-2 income statement from any employer for whom you worked in the previous year

**2.** Your bank statement showing the amount of interest you earned for the previous year. If it's less than ten dollars, you can forget it.

**3.** A copy of your Medical Coverage form. With the new health insurance requirement in place, you must show that you had health coverage for all 12 months in order to avoid a penalty for lack of coverage.

**4.** If you earned income through a business or farm, gather your ledgers or receipts from all income sources throughout the year. Also, keep track of all business expenses, including every item you purchased to help you with your business or farm. If you bought expensive equipment, you'll need to prorate its useful life. I suggest you seek a professional, if that is the case. If you didn't buy anything that needs to be prorated, then simply list the full cost of any items, such as paper, pens, postage, seed, seedling pots, etc, that you purchased in the course of your business.

**Tip:** If you received any Form 1099s, make sure you include that amount as miscellaneous income on your 1040.

### More Advice on Expenditures:

_____

_____

_____

_____

# Chapter Four

## Miscellany

## Emergency Sewing, buttons and rips

If you wind up losing a button or finding a rip in your shirt, you'll want to repair it. Make sure you have an emergency sewing kit. They always come with a couple of buttons, some generic thread and needles, etc. You may also make your own small kit from supplies already on hand. Add a couple of iron on or sew on patches to your kit, for tears in clothing.

### Sewing a Button

When sewing on a new button, you want to make sure it will stay put. Draw a length of thread about two feet long from your spool, cut it, and then thread it through a needle. Once you have it threaded, pull one side of the thread so that it's even with the other side, in order to make a one-foot long, double thread. Tie the thread together at the bottom  in a secure knot, so that the thread won't move as you sew.

Look at your shirt and you will see the spot where the old button was once fastened. Loose bits of thread usually mark the spot, or if not, you can estimate where the button should go, based on the buttonhole. Place the tip of the needle on the INSIDE of the shirt and pull it up through to the outside of the shirt, right where that button used to be. This will leave the ends of the thread (below the knot you made) on the inside of the shirt rather than on the outside.

Now that you have pulled the thread taut, with the knot next to the underside of the shirt and the needle pulled all the way through on the right side of the shirt, place the button on the needle and pull the needle through one of the buttonholes. There are usually either two or four buttonholes on a button, so simply pick one of the holes and slide the button down the thread. Place the button in the spot where it should be attached.

Turn the needle back down and pierce one of the OTHER button holes (not the one you picked to slide the button down, and then pull the needle and thread through it and back down to the underside of the shirt. Pull the needle taught on that side.

Next, you'll have to pull the needle back through the underside into the OTHER button hole (not the one you just used). This might be a bit tricky, since you have to pierce the needle from the underside of the fabric and get it through the hole on the right side of the fabric. The following image shows how you should position your needle, with the thick line below the button representing the fabric:

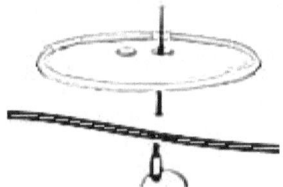

Once you have the needle in the other hole, pull it up through the button and then pull it taught again. Keep doing this at least 6-7 times, back and forth, making sure that you never hit the same buttonhole twice in a row. If you have four holes in your button rather than two, try to space your stitches evenly for a neat look.

When you have only about four inches of thread left, pull the thread through the buttonhole one last time and then pull the thread to the underside of the fabric. Remember, you don't want any knots showing on the right side of the fabric. Either loop the needle through the thread, over and over, and knot it close to the fabric, or else cut the thread very close to the needle, and then tie the loose ends of thread together a couple of times, to make a secure knot. That button should not go anywhere now!

## Fixing a Clothing Tear

If you have access to an iron and ironing board, the easiest method is to use an iron-on fabric patch. Turn the iron on to the hottest setting. If the piece of clothing that is torn is made of a delicate fabric that can't take the heat, make certain you have a cotton cloth on hand, to place over the fabric. If the fabric is made of a tough material, like denim or cotton, you won't need a cloth. Make sure the iron is hot before you begin.

Lay the underside of the fabric you wish to repair flat and facing you on the ironing board. Make sure the fabric lays perfectly flat, with the torn fragments assembled as neatly as possible together. Place the iron-on patch on the underside of the fabric, directly over the tear, with a little bit of the patch overlapping on either side of the tear.

(Note: If you choose a decorative patch to wear on the outside of the garment, then have the right side of the garment facing you.) The shiny side of the iron-on patch goes directly on the torn fabric, while the dull side faces up as you work. Once you've made certain it's perfectly flat and unwrinkled, you're ready to iron.

If the fabric is delicate, gently place a cotton cloth directly over the fabric. Take care not to disturb either your torn fabric or the patch. If the fabric is not delicate, forego this step. Take your hot iron and place it directly over the patch, covering as much of the patch as possible with the hot iron. DO NOT MOVE THE IRON or you will ruin the patch. Press down on the iron with moderate pressure for 15 seconds, or for how many seconds the patch package recommends, without moving the iron.

After 15 seconds, lift the iron and check the sides of the patch. Go over the sides of the patch gently with the iron for another 10-15 seconds if necessary, to ensure a good, secure adhesion.

If you cannot use an iron to repair your tear, then you'll have to sew on a patch. Since sew-on patches will be obvious unless you are an excellent seamstress, you may wish to put the patch on the outside of the fabric and turn it into a design decision. Follow the instructions above for laying the fabric flat, but lay it on the RIGHT side of the fabric, rather than the wrong side. Place the sew-on patch over it with the shiny side down against the torn fabric. Once you've got the patch in the right spot, pin it to the fabric at the top, bottom and sides with straight or safety pins.

Take about three feet of thread and thread your needle as mentioned above for replacing a button. Start on the underside of the fabric and pierce the front side of the fabric right at one corner of the patch. Sew all the way around the top, bottom and sides of the patch, using a "whip stitch" pictured below:

Go all the way around the entire patch, top, bottom and sides, securing the patch to the fabric over the tear. When you are finished, pull the needle to the underside of the fabric, cut the thread close to the needle, and then knot the thread to make the patch secure.

**CHEAP TRICK:** If you have a beloved old pair of jeans or heavy-duty shirt that is falling apart and can't be patched, use duct tape. Hold the tear together and lay the fabric flat, with the underside up. Lay the strip of duct tape firmly along the seam and press down hard. It will hold the garment together through a few more gentle washings. The inside won't be as comfortable as it would have been without the patch, but it will allow you to wear it a few more times. If you'd rather put the duct tape on the outside and make a design out of it, go for it. After all, if people can wear duct tape prom dresses, you can design a duct tape patch!

## Emergency Medicine

### List of Useful Items for your Home Medicine Kit:

(Note: you may need other items, such as a space blanket, if you use your kit for traveling. This is mainly for home use, where you have access to blankets, sheets, etc.)

Flu medication, such as Theraflu
Pepto Bismol  for stomach ailments, nausea
Milk of Magnesia for constipation

Aspirin for pain and muscle aches

Acetaminophen as a fever reducer

Good set of tweezers for pulling out slivers, etc.

Box of plastic bandages (such as "Bandaids.") The one inch wide size is the most useful. Don't get the assorted; you won't use most of them and they'll go to waste.

Capsaicin patch, for back or leg pain. Capsaicin patches get really hot, and they can only be used one time. The Capsaicin is good for when you have to go out. Otherwise, just use a hot water bottle or heating pad. (Be careful with heating pads. If you fall asleep, you could get burned.)

Thermometer, digital

Cough drops

Allergy medication, if needed, such as Claritin

Toothache medicine such as Orajel

Box of gauze and medical tape for larger cuts and scrapes

Pair of scissors to cut gauze.


**Tip:** To ward off colds and flu, take extra Vitamin C during the cold season.


**Important:** Don't mix medicines. If you've already taken Theraflu, for example, don't also take an aspirin. Wait the appropriate amount of time mentioned on the box before trying something else. If you are suffering from two different ailments, such as a stomach ache and a cough, you might take Pepto Bismol and a cough drop. Or, you may take an aspirin for pain plus rub a little Orajel on an aching tooth. Always check with Drugs.com or another website, however, before taking two different medicines, as there may be negative interactions between drugs.

**Customized Health Information:**

_____

_____

_____

_____

_____

_____

# Death: What do I do if someone dies?

If you are the one in charge when someone dies, the following are the steps you must take. Please give yourself a few hours to absorb everything, and if someone asks if they can help, delegate some of these tasks to them.

You should obtain power of attorney for your elders long before they die, if possible. That way, you'll have access to banks, taxes, mortgages, etc, and the transition will flow more smoothly.

The first thing you must do is to arrange for organ donation, if the person wished their organs to be used to benefit others. This must be done immediately or the organs will be useless. If the person died in the hospital, then there will be someone available to walk you through this process. Just ask the nurse or doctor. If the person died outside the hospital, then contact the nearest hospital and ask them what to do.

After you've called immediate family members who may want to pay their last respects, choose a funeral home to transport the body from the morgue to its facility. The best funeral home to use in your own home town is:

If you are living in a new area, check the Better Business Bureau website at bbb.org and look up "funeral homes" in your town. Pick one with a good rating.

Lock up your deceased loved one's property and car. If the home will be vacant now that the loved one is gone, make sure pets are cared for. Notify the post office to redirect mail to your home, so that you can check the mail for bills, subscriptions, etc. This will give you an idea of what bills need to be cancelled. It may also give you insight into any unknown friends of the deceased that may wish to know of the person's death.

Stop all health insurance, dental insurance, life insurance payments, and all other bills that are no longer relevant. By forwarding the mail, you may find out some of these, but if the deceased paid many bills online, you may need to view those at the bank. Make sure you close all credit card accounts immediately.

Arrange a meeting with the funeral director at the funeral home. Decide if there will be a service, or if the body will be cremated. If the deceased has expressed no wishes in this matter and you do not have a lot of money, then I would choose the cheapest option to avoid unnecessary expense. Do what you think best, but don't let yourself be talked into a more expensive service than you can afford. If you feel as if you might be intimidated into choosing an expensive option, take a cheapskate friend with you to the funeral home. They'll keep you from spending too much money.

If your loved one was a military veteran, go to the Veteran's Affairs website and ask for information on a military funeral. You may also ask about veteran's benefits that may help you.

You will have to obtain copies of the death certificate, in order to present to banks, mortgage companies, and life insurance companies. The funeral director will be able to help you secure these copies. Purchase between 5-10 or even more, depending upon how many different bank accounts, life insurance policies, etc, the person owned.

Once you have obtained the death certificates, locate all of the deceased's paperwork, such as bank records and life insurance. Write to each one, phone them, email them, or go in person to speak to them, bringing a copy of the death certificate. If you don't have power of attorney, you will need authorization from any other heirs to act as the executor. If you believe there will be contention among the siblings, hire an attorney that specializes in estates. Otherwise, just seek appointments with these companies and send them copies of the death certificate and your authorization, as power of attorney or in consensus with your relatives, to handle all the finances.

You'll also need to contact the Social Security office to stop all checks coming to the deceased. The last check they earned, for the month that they died, is the property of the heirs. Any checks that are accidentally sent after that should be returned to the Social Security Administration. Contact Medicare, as well, to inform them of the person's death.

If you wish to have a funeral service or a gathering, you'll have to decide on the date and time, in conjunction with the funeral director. If you are burying the deceased rather than cremating, you'll have to arrange for a burial plot, a headstone, etc.

Once you decide on arrangements or gatherings, prepare an obituary for the local newspaper and Facebook, if the deceased was a member of Facebook. If there is a will, it will have to be followed. Make sure to send thank you notes to anyone who expressed their condolences, in order to assure them that their warm wishes were received and appreciated.

One of the last things you will do is file a final tax return for the individual, if they were working at the time of death or earned enough income to qualify for filing a tax return (or even if they didn't, if you suspect they would get a tax refund that can go to the heirs). Also notify the elections board to take them off the voter rolls.

While there are many other things that may come up, these are the most vital. You won't be able to get all of them done in the first week, but try to finish everything within a month. Take time to absorb everything, and if you need help, contact a bereavement counselor or an attorney.

## Other Useful Tidbits

The following is a list of random tips and tricks, some very important, some not so much, that I have learned in every day life. I hope you find them as useful as I have.

**Electrical Tip:** Never run two energy-hog small appliances, such as an electric griddle and a microwave or a toaster oven, at the same time in adjacent or nearby sockets. In houses or apartments with inadequate wiring, you may blow a fuse and they'll both go out. Better to turn off one in order to use the other.

**Tip for cutting down on dishes:**

If you need a lot of little bits of food, such as chopped onions, carrots and such for a meal, you can use a muffin tin and fill each cup with one item, and serve it that way. You won't have as many dishes to wash.

**Travel Tip:** If you are ever lost and need directions, the best place to find them is from a pizza place that delivers.

**Filling water bottles:** If you don't want your water to get warm during the day when you're out working or playing, just fill your personal water bottle with an inch or two of water at night and put it in your freezer. In the morning, fill it up the rest of the way with water, and it will stay nice and cold for a lot longer.

## Natural Pest Control:

**How to get rid of ants:**

In a small bowl, make a paste of ¼ cup honey or agave nectar, 1 tablespoon of cornstarch (in the cabinet with the spices) and a plastic spoon full of borax (borax is a laundry booster, so you will find it with the detergents and bleach).  Stir all ingredients well and spread it on a cardboard or paper. Leave it out near the ants. Within a few hours, it will attract and then kill all the ants. Make sure you use a separate plastic spoon for the borax. Don't try to wash it or let it touch anything else; borax kills the ants, after all, and it's not good for you to ingest, either!

**How to get rid of slugs in a garden:**

Slugs love beer. If you put out a small pan of beer at night near plants that slugs have infested, you may find that there are drowned slugs when you go out in the morning.

**How to rid an area of mice:**

Mice hate peppermint. Crush peppermint leaves and leave them in areas where mice are suspected.

**What to do if you see roaches:**

Roaches are just about the worst vermin of human existence. When you see one, you can bet there will be a hundred more lurking in the woodwork. To get rid of them without calling a pesticide company, get a plastic cup and fill it with three parts of boric acid or borax (mentioned above for ants) and one part of powdered sugar. Use a plastic spoon to mix it thoroughly. Add some warm water so that you can mix it into a paste. Place a spoonful on a 3x5 card or any piece of cardboard, and slide these pieces of cardboard under furniture, inside cabinets, etc. If you have pets, keep these items OUT OF THE REACH of the pets. They may get sick from the borax.

If that fails, then get a big jug of diatomaceous earth and sprinkle that in all the cracks, inside the cabinets, and anywhere where there will be roaches. Diatomaceous earth is not harmful to humans or pets, although it would irritate your feet if you walked on it. Sprinkle it in out of the way places where bugs love to congregate.

### Mom's Most Useful Tips:

_____

_____

_____

_____

_____

# Personal Message from Mom

In this spot, moms of the world should write their own message to their offspring. After you're gone, Mom, your adult children will treasure the words you leave them and the love that you show them. They may even pass them on to your future grandchildren and great-grandchildren. So make the words count and speak from your heart; that's all a son or daughter really needs from you.

_____

_____

_____

_____

_____

_____

## About the Author

Born in the inner-city Pilsen district of Chicago, Kathleen Rita Cook spent her youth writing fiction, studying Irish mythology and dreaming of becoming a nun. Her mother worked on the South Water Market while she and her sister attended St. Procopius Catholic School. The family eventually ended up in Phoenix, where Katy spent forty years raising four children, writing, editing, and volunteering in local schools and churches. After nearly half a century in the desert, Katy plans to return to her roots in the Midwest.

www.ingramcontent.com/pod-product-compliance
Lightning Source LLC
Chambersburg PA
CBHW030441290526
45786CB00001B/396